As You Like It

As You Like It

William Shakespeare

Illustrated by
Hugh Thomson

Gramercy Books
New York • Avenel, New Jersey

Preface and Compilation
Copyright © 1993 by Outlet Book Company, Inc.
All rights reserved

This 1993 edition is published by Gramercy Books
distributed by Outlet Book Company, Inc.,
a Random House Company,
40 Engelhard Avenue
Avenel, New Jersey 07001

The text used in this edition was
originally published in
The New Temple Shakespeare series,
edited by M.R. Ridley

Designed by Melissa Ring

Random House
New York • Toronto • London • Sydney • Auckland

Printed and bound in Singapore

Library of Congress Cataloging-in-Publication Data
Shakespeare, William, 1564–1616.
As you like it / by William Shakespeare.
p. :   ;   cm. — (Illustrated Shakespeare)
ISBN 0-517-06489-8
I. Title.   II. Series: Shakespeare, William, 1564–1616.
Illustrated Shakespeare.
PR2803.A1   1993   92-38745
822.3′3—dc20   CIP

8 7 6 5 4 3 2 1

PREFACE

As You Like It ranks alongside *A Midsummer Night's Dream* and *Twelfth Night* as one of William Shakespeare's great comedies. It is a love story filled with whimsy and engaging wordplay exchanged by Rosalind, disguised as a boy, and Orlando as they roam the idyllic forest of Arden.

Written between the historical plays and the tragedies, *As You Like It* is certainly Shakespeare's sunniest play. It has great warmth and is peopled with good-hearted and memorable characters. Rosalind, courageous, high-spirited, and truly witty, is the most universally loved of all Shakespeare's heroines. And Touchstone, who is the mellowest of cynical jesters, provides a dash of acid reality.

Many of Shakespeare's plays were first published individually in Quarto editions that were later collected and published in Folio editions. But the only source for *As You Like It* is the first Folio edition of 1623. The text of this edition is the nearest possible approximation to what Shakespeare actually wrote. To avoid distraction, however, the spelling has been modernized. The punctuation adheres closely to the Elizabethan punctuation of the early text and, therefore, is often indicative of the way in which the lines are to be spoken.

The charming illustrations were done by Hugh Thomson, one of the most popular and influential of Edwardian illustrators. His lighthearted, sensitive watercolors and whimsical black and white drawings evoke the atmosphere of the pastoral woodland scenes and add a delightful dimension to this sprightly play.

GAIL HARVEY

New York
1993

DRAMATIS PERSONAE

DUKE, *living in banishment.*
FREDERICK, *his brother, and usurper of his dominions.*
AMIENS,
JAQUES, } *lords attending on the banished Duke.*
LE BEAU, *a courtier attending on Frederick.*
CHARLES, *wrestler to Frederick.*
OLIVER,
JAQUES, } *sons of Sir Rowland de Boys.*
ORLANDO,
ADAM,
DENNIS, } *servants to Oliver.*
TOUCHSTONE, *a clown.*
SIR OLIVER MARTEXT, *a vicar.*
CORIN,
SILVIUS, } *shepherds.*
WILLIAM, *a country fellow, in love with Audrey.*
A person representing Hymen.

ROSALIND, *daughter to the banished Duke.*
CELIA, *daughter to Frederick.*
PHEBE, *a shepherdess.*
AUDREY, *a country wench.*

Lords, pages, and attendants, &c.

SCENE: *Oliver's house; Duke Frederick's court; and the Forest of Arden.*

ACT
1

SCENE I

Orchard of Oliver's house

Enter Orlando and Adam

Orlando. As I remember, Adam, it was upon this fashion bequeathed me by will, but poor a thousand crowns, and, as thou sayest, charged my brother, on his blessing, to breed me well: and there begins my sadness. My brother Jaques he keeps at school, and report speaks goldenly of his profit: for my part, he keeps me rustically at home, or (to speak more properly) stays me here at home unkept; for call you that keeping for a gentleman of my birth, that differs not from the stalling of an ox? His horses are bred better, for, besides that they are fair with their feeding, they are taught their manage, and to that end riders dearly hired: but I, his brother, gain nothing under him but growth, for the which his animals on his dunghills are as much bound to him as I. Besides this nothing that he so plentifully gives me, the something that nature gave me his countenance seems to take from me: he lets me feed with his hinds, bars me the place of a brother, and, as much as in him lies, mines my gentility with my education. This is it, Adam, that grieves me, and the spirit of my father, which I think is within me, begins to mutiny against this servitude. I will no longer endure it, though yet I know no wise remedy how to avoid it.

Adam. Yonder comes my master, your brother.

Orlando. Go apart, Adam, and thou shalt hear how he will shake me up.

Enter Oliver

Oliver. Now, sir! what make you here?

Orlando. Nothing: I am not taught to make any thing.

Oliver. What mar you then, sir?

Orlando. Marry, sir, I am helping you to mar that which God made, a poor unworthy brother of yours, with idleness.

Oliver. Marry, sir, be better employed, and be naught awhile.

Orlando. Shall I keep your hogs, and eat husks with them? What prodigal portion have I spent, that I should come to such penury?

Oliver. Know you where you are, sir?

Orlando. O, sir, very well; here in your orchard.

Oliver. Know you before whom, sir?

Orlando. Ay, better than him I am before knows me. I know you are my eldest brother, and in the gentle condition of blood you should so know me. The courtesy of nations allows you my better, in that you are the first-born, but the same tradition takes not away my blood, were there twenty brothers betwixt us: I have as much of my father in me as you, albeit I confess your coming before me is nearer to his reverence.

Oliver. What, boy!   *Strikes him*

Orlando. Come, come, elder brother, you are too young in this.

Oliver. Wilt thou lay hands on me, villain?

Orlando. I am no villain; I am the youngest son of Sir Rowland de Boys; he was my father, and he is thrice a villain that says such a father begot villains. Wert thou not my brother, I would not take this hand from thy throat till this other had pulled out thy tongue for saying so: thou hast railed on thyself.

Adam. Sweet masters, be patient: for your father's remembrance, be at accord.

Oliver. Let me go, I say.

Orlando. I will not, till I please: you shall hear me. My father charged you in his will to give me good education: you have trained me like a peasant, obscuring and hiding from me all gentlemanlike qualities. The spirit of my father grows strong in me, and I will no longer endure it: therefore allow me such exercises as may become a gentleman, or give me the poor allottery my father left me by testament; with that I will go buy my fortunes.

Oliver. And what wilt thou do? beg, when that is spent? Well, sir, get you in: I will not long be troubled with you; you shall have some part of your will: I pray you, leave me.

Orlando. I will no further offend you than becomes me for my good.

Oliver. Get you with him, you old dog.

Adam. Is 'old dog' my reward? Most true, I have lost my teeth in your service. God be with my old master! he would not have spoke such a word.

Exeunt Orlando and Adam

Oliver. Is it even so? begin you to grow upon me? I will physic your rankness, and yet give no thousand crowns neither. Holla, Dennis!

Enter Dennis

Dennis. Calls your worship?

Oliver. Was not Charles, the Duke's wrestler, here to speak with me?

Dennis. So please you, he is here at the door, and importunes access to you.

Oliver. Call him in. (*exit Dennis.*) 'Twill be a good way; and to-morrow the wrestling is.

Enter Charles

Charles. Good morrow to your worship.

Oliver. Good Monsieur Charles, what's the new news at the new court?

Charles. There's no news at the court, sir, but the old news: that is, the old Duke is banished by his younger brother the new Duke; and three or four loving lords have put themselves into voluntary exile with him, whose lands and revenues enrich the new Duke; therefore he gives them good leave to wander.

Oliver. Can you tell if Rosalind, the Duke's daughter, be banished with her father?

Charles. O, no; for the Duke's daughter, her cousin, so loves her, being ever from their cradles bred together, that she would have followed her exile, or have died to stay behind her. She is at the court, and no less beloved of her uncle than his own daughter; and never two ladies loved as they do.

Oliver. Where will the old Duke live?

Charles. They say he is already in the forest of Arden, and a many merry men with him; and there they live like the old Robin Hood of England: they say many young gentlemen flock to him every day, and fleet the time carelessly as they did in the golden world.

Oliver. What, you wrestle to-morrow before the new Duke?

Charles. Marry, do I, sir; and I came to acquaint you with a matter. I am given, sir, secretly to understand that your younger brother, Orlando, hath a disposition to come in disguised against me to try a fall. To-morrow, sir, I wrestle for my credit, and he that escapes me without some broken limb shall acquit him well: your brother is but young and tender, and for your love I would be loath to foil him, as I must for my own honour if he come in: therefore, out of my love to you, I came hither to acquaint you withal, that either you might stay him from his intendment, or brook such disgrace well as he shall run into, in that it is a thing of his own search, and altogether against my will.

Oliver. Charles, I thank thee for thy love to me, which thou shalt find I will most kindly requite. I had myself notice of my brother's purpose herein, and have by underhand means laboured to dissuade him from it: but he is resolute. I'll tell thee, Charles, it is the stubbornest young fellow of France, full of ambition, an envious emulator of every man's good parts, a secret and villanous contriver against me his natural brother: therefore use thy discretion; I had as lief thou didst break his neck as his finger. And thou wert best look to 't; for if thou dost him any slight disgrace, or if he do not mightily grace himself on thee, he will practice against thee by poison, entrap thee by some treacherous device, and never leave thee till he hath ta'en thy life by some indirect means or other; for I assure thee (and almost with tears I speak it) there is not one so young and so villanous this day living. I speak but brotherly of him; but should I anatomize him to thee, as he is, I must blush, and weep, and thou must look pale and wonder.

Charles. I am heartily glad I came hither to you. If he come to-morrow, I'll give him his payment: if ever he go alone again, I'll never wrestle for prize more: and so, God keep your worship!

Oliver. Farewell, good Charles. (*exit Charles.*) Now will I stir this gamester: I hope I shall see an end of him; for my soul (yet I know not why) hates nothing more than he. Yet he's gentle, never schooled, and yet learned, full of noble device, of all sorts enchantingly beloved, and indeed so much in the heart of the world, and especially of my own people, who best know him, that I am altogether misprised: but it shall not be so long, this wrestler shall clear all: nothing remains but that I kindle the boy thither, which now I'll go about.   *Exit*

SCENE II

Enter Rosalind and Celia

Celia. I pray thee, Rosalind, sweet my coz, be merry.

Rosalind. Dear Celia, I show more mirth than I am mistress of; and would you yet I were merrier? Unless you could teach me to forget a banished father, you must not learn me how to remember any extraordinary pleasure.

Celia. Herein I see thou lovest me not with the full weight that I love thee. If my uncle, thy banished father, had banished thy uncle, the Duke my father, so thou hadst been still with me, I could have taught my love to take thy father for mine: so wouldst thou, if the truth of thy love to me were so righteously tempered as mine is to thee.

Rosalind. Well, I will forget the condition of my estate, to rejoice in yours.

Celia. You know my father hath no child but I, nor none is like to have; and, truly, when he dies, thou shalt be his heir; for what he hath taken away from thy father perforce, I will render thee again in affection; by mine honour, I will, and when I break that oath, let me turn monster: therefore, my sweet Rose, my dear Rose, be merry.

Rosalind. From henceforth I will, coz, and devise sports. Let me see; what think you of falling in love?

Celia. Marry, I prithee, do, to make sport withal: but love no man in good earnest, nor no further in sport neither, than with safety of a pure blush thou mayst in honour come off again.

Rosalind. What shall be our sport, then?

Celia. Let us sit and mock the good housewife Fortune from

her wheel, that her gifts may henceforth be bestowed equally.

Rosalind. I would we could do so; for her benefits are mightily misplaced, and the bountiful blind woman doth most mistake in her gifts to women.

Celia. 'Tis true, for those that she makes fair she scarce makes honest, and those that she makes honest she makes very ill-favouredly.

Rosalind. Nay, now thou goest from Fortune's office to Nature's: Fortune reigns in gifts of the world, not in the lineaments of Nature.

Enter Touchstone

Celia. No? when Nature hath made a fair creature, may she not by Fortune fall into the fire? Though Nature hath given us wit to flout at Fortune, hath not Fortune sent in this fool to cut off the argument?

Rosalind. Indeed, there is Fortune too hard for Nature, when Fortune makes Nature's natural the cutter-off of Nature's wit.

Celia. Peradventure this is not Fortune's work neither, but Nature's; who perceiveth our natural wits too dull to reason of such goddesses, hath sent this natural for our whetstone; for always the dulness of the fool is the whetstone of the wits. How now, wit! whither wander you?

Touchstone. Mistress, you must come away to your father.

Celia. Were you made the messenger?

Touchstone. No, by mine honour, but I was bid to come for you.

Rosalind. Where learned you that oath, fool?

Touchstone. Of a certain knight, that swore by his honour they were good pancakes, and swore by his honour the mustard was naught; now I'll stand to it, the pancakes were naught, and the mustard was good, and yet was not the knight forsworn.

Celia. How prove you that in the great heap of your knowledge?

Rosalind. Ay, marry, now unmuzzle your wisdom.

Touchstone. Stand you both forth now: stroke your chins, and swear by your beards that I am a knave.

Celia. By our beards (if we had them) thou art.

Touchstone. By my knavery (if I had it) then I were; but if you swear by that that is not, you are not forsworn: no more was this knight swearing by his honour, for he never had any; or if he had, he had sworn it away, before ever he saw those pancakes, or that mustard.

Celia. Prithee, who is 't that thou meanest?

Touchstone. One that old Frederick, your father, loves.

Celia. My father's love is enough to honour him: enough! speak no more of him; you'll be whipped for taxation one of these days.

Touchstone. The more pity, that fools may not speak wisely what wise men do foolishly.

Celia. By my troth, thou sayest true; for since the little wit that fools have was silenced, the little foolery that wise men have makes a great show. Here comes Monsieur Le Beau.

Rosalind. With his mouth full of news.

Celia. Which he will put on us, as pigeons feed their young.

Rosalind. Then shall we be news-crammed.

Celia. All the better; we shall be the more marketable.

Enter Le Beau

Bon jour, Monsieur Le Beau; what's the news?

Le Beau. Fair princess, you have lost much good sport.

Celia. Sport? of what colour?

Le Beau. What colour, madam! how shall I answer you?

Rosalind. As wit and fortune will.

Touchstone. Or as the Destinies decrees.

Celia. Well said: that was laid on with a trowel.

Touchstone. Nay, if I keep not my rank,—

Rosalind. Thou losest thy old smell.

Le Beau. You amaze me, ladies: I would have told you of good wrestling, which you have lost the sight of.

Rosalind. Yet tell us the manner of the wrestling.

Le Beau. I will tell you the beginning; and, if it please your ladyships, you may see the end, for the best is yet to do, and here, where you are, they are coming to perform it.

Celia. Well, the beginning that is dead and buried.

Le Beau. There comes an old man and his three sons,—

Celia. I could match this beginning with an old tale.

Le Beau. Three proper young men, of excellent growth and presence.

Rosalind. With bills on their necks, 'Be it known unto all men by these presents.'

Le Beau. The eldest of the three wrestled with Charles, the Duke's wrestler, which Charles in a moment threw him, and broke three of his ribs, that there is little hope of life in him: so he served the second, and so the third. Yonder they lie, the poor old man, their father, making such pitiful dole over them that all the beholders take his part with weeping.

Rosalind. Alas!

Touchstone. But what is the sport, monsieur, that the ladies have lost?

Le Beau. Why, this that I speak of.

Touchstone. Thus men may grow wiser every day: it is the first time that ever I heard breaking of ribs was sport for ladies.

Celia. Or I, I promise thee.

Rosalind. But is there any else longs to see this broken music in his sides? is there yet another dotes upon rib-breaking? Shall we see this wrestling, cousin?

Le Beau. You must if you stay here, for here is the place appointed for the wrestling, and they are ready to perform it.

Celia. Yonder, sure, they are coming: let us now stay and see it.

Flourish. Enter Duke Frederick, Lords, Orlando, Charles, and Attendants

Duke Frederick. Come on: since the youth will not be entreated, his own peril on his forwardness.

Rosalind. Is yonder the man?

Le Beau. Even he, madam.

Celia. Alas, he is too young! yet he looks successfully.

Duke Frederick. How now, daughter, and cousin; are you crept hither to see the wrestling?

Rosalind. Ay, my liege, so please you give us leave.

Duke Frederick. You will take little delight in it, I can tell you, there is such odds in the man. In pity of the challenger's youth I would fain dissuade him, but he will not be entreated. Speak to him, ladies, see if you can move him.

Celia. Call him hither, good Monsieur Le Beau.

Duke Frederick. Do so: I'll not be by.

Le Beau. Monsieur the challenger, the princess calls for you.

Orlando. I attend them with all respect and duty.

Rosalind. Young man, have you challenged Charles the wrestler?

Orlando. No, fair princess; he is the general challenger: I come but in as others do, to try with him the strength of my youth.

Celia. Young gentleman, your spirits are too bold for your years. You have seen cruel proof of this man's strength: if you saw yourself with your eyes, or knew yourself with your judgement, the fear of your adventure would counsel you to a more equal enterprise. We pray you for your own sake to embrace your own safety, and give over this attempt.

Rosalind. Do, young sir; your reputation shall not therefore be misprised: we will make it our suit to the Duke that the wrestling might not go forward.

Orlando. I beseech you, punish me not with your hard thoughts, wherein I confess me much guilty to deny so fair and excellent ladies any thing. But let your fair eyes and gentle wishes go with me to my trial: wherein if I be foiled, there is but one shamed that was never gracious; if killed, but one dead that is willing to be so: I shall do my friends no wrong, for I have none to lament me; the world no injury, for in it I have nothing: only in the world I fill up a place, which may be better supplied, when I have made it empty.

Rosalind. The little strength that I have, I would it were with you.

Celia. And mine to eke out hers.

Rosalind. Fare you well: pray heaven I be deceived in you!

Celia. Your heart's desires be with you!

Charles. Come, where is this young gallant that is so desirous to lie with his mother earth?

Orlando. Ready, sir; but his will hath in it a more modest working.

Duke Frederick. You shall try but one fall.

Charles. No, I warrant your Grace you shall not entreat him to a second, that have so mightily persuaded him from a first.

Orlando. You mean to mock me after; you should not have mocked me before: but come your ways.

Rosalind. Now Hercules be thy speed, young man!

Celia. I would I were invisible, to catch the strong fellow by the leg.   *They wrestle*

Rosalind. O excellent young man!

Celia. If I had a thunderbolt in mine eye, I can tell who should down.   *Shout. Charles is thrown*

Duke Frederick. No more, no more.

Orlando. Yes, I beseech your Grace, I am not yet well breath'd.

Duke Frederick. How dost thou, Charles?

Le Beau. He cannot speak, my lord.

Duke Frederick. Bear him away. What is thy name, young
    man?

Orlando. Orlando, my liege, the youngest son of Sir Rowland de Boys.

Duke Frederick. I would thou hadst been son to some man
    else:
  The world esteem'd thy father honourable,
  But I did find him still mine enemy:
  Thou shouldst have better pleas'd me with this deed,
  Hadst thou descended from another house:
  But fair thee well, thou art a gallant youth;
  I would thou hadst told me of another father.
                Exeunt Duke Frederick, train, and Le Beau

Celia. Were I my father, coz, would I do this?

Orlando. I am more proud to be Sir Rowland's son,
  His youngest son, and would not change that calling
  To be adopted heir to Frederick.

Rosalind. My father lov'd Sir Rowland as his soul,
  And all the world was of my father's mind:
  Had I before known this young man his son,
  I should have given him tears unto entreaties,
  Ere he should thus have ventur'd.

Celia.   Gentle cousin,
  Let us go thank him, and encourage him:
  My father's rough and envious disposition
  Sticks me at heart. Sir, you have well deserv'd:
  If you do keep your promises in love,
  But justly as you have exceeded all promise,
  Your mistress shall be happy.

Rosalind.   Gentleman,
             Giving him a chain from her neck
  Wear this for me; one out of suits with fortune,
  That could give more, but that her hand lacks means.
  Shall we go, coz?

Celia.   Ay. Fare you well, fair gentleman.

Orlando. Can I not say, I thank you? My better parts
    Are all thrown down, and that which here stands up
    Is but a quintain, a mere lifeless block.

Rosalind. He calls us back: my pride fell with my fortunes;
    I'll ask him what he would. Did you call, sir?
    Sir, you have wrestled well, and overthrown
    More than your enemies.

Celia.   Will you go, coz?

Rosalind. Have with you: fare you well.

                              Exeunt Rosalind and Celia

Orlando. What passion hangs these weights upon my
        tongue?
    I cannot speak to her, yet she urged conference.
    O poor Orlando, thou art overthrown!
    Or Charles, or something weaker, masters thee.

                    Re-enter Le Beau

Le Beau. Good sir, I do in friendship counsel you
    To leave this place. Albeit you have deserv'd
    High commendation, true applause, and love,
    Yet such is now the Duke's condition,
    That he misconsters all that you have done:
    The Duke is humorous; what he is, indeed,
    More suits you to conceive than I to speak of.

Orlando. I thank you, sir: and pray you tell me this,
    Which of the two was daughter of the Duke,
    That here was at the wrestling?

Le Beau. Neither his daughter, if we judge by manners,
    But yet, indeed, the taller is his daughter;
    The other is daughter to the banish'd Duke,
    And here detain'd by her usurping uncle
    To keep his daughter company, whose loves
    Are dearer than the natural bond of sisters:
    But I can tell you that of late this Duke
    Hath ta'en displeasure 'gainst his gentle niece,

Grounded upon no other argument
But that the people praise her for her virtues,
And pity her, for her good father's sake;
And, on my life, his malice 'gainst the lady
Will suddenly break forth. Sir, fare you well;
Hereafter in a better world than this,
I shall desire more love and knowledge of you.

Orlando. I rest much bounden to you: fare you well.

Exit Le Beau

Thus must I from the smoke into the smother,
From tyrant Duke, unto a tyrant brother:
But heavenly Rosalind!   *Exit*

SCENE III

A room in the palace

Enter Celia and Rosalind

Celia. Why, cousin! why, Rosalind! Cupid have mercy! not
a word?

Rosalind. Not one to throw at a dog.

Celia. No, thy words are too precious to be cast away upon
curs; throw some of them at me; come lame me with
reasons.

Rosalind. Then there were two cousins laid up, when the
one should be lamed with reasons, and the other mad
without any.

Celia. But is all this for your father?

Rosalind. No, some of it is for my child's father. O, how
full of briers is this working-day world!

Celia. They are but burs, cousin, thrown upon thee in holiday foolery; if we walk not in the trodden paths, our very petticoats will catch them.

Rosalind. I could shake them off my coat; these burs are in my heart.

Celia. Hem them away.

Rosalind. I would try if I could cry hem, and have him.

Celia. Come, come, wrestle with thy affections.

Rosalind. O, they take the part of a better wrestler than myself!

Celia. O, a good wish upon you! you will try in time, in despite of a fall. But, turning these jests out of service, let us talk in good earnest: is it possible, on such a sudden, you should fall into so strong a liking with old Sir Rowland's youngest son?

Rosalind. The Duke my father loved his father dearly.

Celia. Doth it therefore ensue that you should love his son dearly? By this kind of chase, I should hate him, for my father hated his father dearly; yet I hate not Orlando.

Rosalind. No, faith, hate him not, for my sake.

Celia. Why should I not? doth he not deserve well?

Rosalind. Let me love him for that, and do you love him because I do. Look, here comes the Duke.

Celia. With his eyes full of anger.

Enter Duke Frederick, with Lords

Duke Frederick. Mistress, dispatch you with your safest haste,
And get you from our court.

Rosalind.   Me, uncle?

Duke Frederick.   You, cousin,
Within these ten days if that thou be'st found
So near our public court as twenty miles,
Thou diest for it.

Rosalind.   I do beseech your Grace,
Let me the knowledge of my fault bear with me:

If with myself I hold intelligence,
Or have acquaintance with mine own desires,
If that I do not dream, or be not frantic,—
As I do trust I am not,—then, dear uncle,
Never so much as in a thought unborn
Did I offend your Highness.
Duke Frederick.   Thus do all traitors:
If their purgation did consist in words,
They are as innocent as grace itself:
Let it suffice thee that I trust thee not.
Rosalind. Yet your mistrust cannot make me a traitor:
Tell me whereon the likelihood depends.
Duke Frederick. Thou art thy father's daughter, there's
enough.
Rosalind. So was I when your Highness took his dukedom,
So was I when your Highness banish'd him:
Treason is not inherited, my lord,
Or, if we did derive it from our friends,
What's that to me? my father was no traitor:
Then, good my liege, mistake me not so much
To think my poverty is treacherous.
Celia. Dear sovereign, hear me speak.
Duke Frederick. Ay, Celia; we stay'd her for your sake,
Else had she with her father rang'd along.
Celia. I did not then entreat to have her stay,
It was your pleasure, and your own remorse;
I was too young that time to value her,
But now I know her: if she be a traitor,
Why so am I; we still have slept together,
Rose at an instant, learn'd, play'd, ate together,
And wheresoe'er we went, like Juno's swans,
Still we went coupled and inseparable.
Duke Frederick. She is too subtle for thee; and her smooth-
ness,
Her very silence, and her patience,
Speak to the people, and they pity her.

Thou art a fool, she robs thee of thy name,
And thou wilt show more bright, and seem more virtuous,
When she is gone. Then open not thy lips:
Firm and irrevocable is my doom,
Which I have pass'd upon her; she is banish'd.
Celia. Pronounce that sentence then on me, my liege;
I cannot live out of her company.
Duke Frederick. You are a fool. You, niece, provide your-
self;
If you outstay the time, upon mine honour,
And in the greatness of my word, you die.

       Exeunt Duke Frederick and Lords

Celia. O my poor Rosalind, whither wilt thou go?
Wilt thou change fathers? I will give thee mine.
I charge thee, be not thou more griev'd than I am.
Rosalind. I have more cause.
Celia.   Thou hast not, cousin;
Prithee, be cheerful: know'st thou not the Duke
Hath banish'd me, his daughter?
Rosalind.   That he hath not.
Celia. No, hath not? Rosalind lacks then the love
Which teacheth thee that thou and I am one:
Shall we be sunder'd? shall we part, sweet girl?
No, let my father seek another heir:
Therefore devise with me how we may fly,
Whither to go, and what to bear with us,
And do not seek to take your change upon you,
To bear your griefs yourself, and leave me out;
For by this heaven, now at our sorrows pale,
Say what thou canst, I'll go along with thee.
Rosalind. Why, whither shall we go?
Celia. To seek my uncle in the forest of Arden.
Rosalind. Alas, what danger will it be to us,
(Maids as we are) to travel forth so far?
Beauty provoketh thieves sooner than gold.
Celia. I'll put myself in poor and mean attire,

And with a kind of umber smirch my face;
The like do you: so shall we pass along,
And never stir assailants.

Rosalind.   Were it not better,
Because that I am more than common tall,
That I did suit me all points like a man,
A gallant curtle-axe upon my thigh,
A boar-spear in my hand? and—in my heart
Lie there what hidden woman's fear there will—
We'll have a swashing and a martial outside,
As many other mannish cowards have,
That do outface it with their semblances.

Celia. What shall I call thee when thou art a man?

Rosalind. I'll have no worse a name than Jove's own page,
And therefore look you call me Ganymede;
But what will you be call'd?

Celia. Something that hath a reference to my state:
No longer Celia, but Aliena.

Rosalind. But, cousin, what if we assay'd to steal
The clownish fool out of your father's court?
Would he not be a comfort to our travel?

Celia. He'll go along o'er the wide world with me
Leave me alone to woo him. Let's away,
And get our jewels and our wealth together,
Devise the fittest time, and safest way
To hide us from pursuit that will be made
After my flight. Now go we in content
To liberty, and not to banishment.   *Exeunt*

ACT II

SCENE I

The Forest of Arden

Enter Duke senior, Amiens, and two or three
Lords, like foresters

Duke Sr. Now, my co-mates, and brothers in exile,
Hath not old custom made this life more sweet
Than that of painted pomp? Are not these woods
More free from peril than the envious court?
Here feel we not the penalty of Adam,
The seasons' difference? as the icy fang
And churlish chiding of the winter's wind,
Which, when it bites and blows upon my body,
Even till I shrink with cold, I smile, and say
'This is no flattery: these are counsellors
That feelingly persuade me what I am.'
Sweet are the uses of adversity,
Which, like the toad, ugly and venomous,
Wears yet a precious jewel in his head:
And this our life, exempt from public haunt,
Finds tongues in trees, books in the running brooks,
Sermons in stones, and good in every thing.
I would not change it.
Amiens.   Happy is your Grace,
That can translate the stubbornness of fortune
Into so quiet and so sweet a style.
Duke Sr. Come, shall we go and kill us venison?
And yet it irks me the poor dappled fools,
Being native burghers of this desert city,
Should in their own confines with forked heads
Have their round haunches gored.
First Lord.   Indeed, my lord,
The melancholy Jaques grieves at that,
And, in that kind, swears you do more usurp
Than doth your brother that hath banish'd you.

    To-day my Lord of Amiens, and myself,
    Did steal behind him as he lay along
    Under an oak, whose antique root peeps out
    Upon the brook that brawls along this wood,
    To the which place a poor sequester'd stag,
    That from the hunter's aim had ta'en a hurt,
    Did come to languish; and indeed, my lord,
    The wretched animal heav'd forth such groans,
    That their discharge did stretch his leathern coat
    Almost to bursting, and the big round tears
    Cours'd one another down his innocent nose
    In piteous chase: and thus the hairy fool,
    Much marked of the melancholy Jaques,
    Stood on the extremest verge of the swift brook,
    Augmenting it with tears.
Duke Sr.   But what said Jaques?
    Did he not moralise this spectacle?
First Lord. O, yes, into a thousand similes.
    First, for his weeping into the needless stream;
    'Poor deer,' quoth he, 'thou mak'st a testament
    As worldlings do, giving thy sum of more
    To that which had too much:' then, being there alone,
    Left and abandon'd of his velvet friends;
    ' 'Tis right,' quoth he; 'thus misery doth part
    The flux of company:' anon a careless herd,
    Full of the pasture, jumps along by him
    And never stays to greet him; 'Ay,' quoth Jaques,
    'Sweep on, you fat and greasy citizens;
    'Tis just the fashion: wherefore do you look
    Upon that poor and broken bankrupt there?'
    Thus most invectively he pierceth through
    The body of the country, city, court,
    Yea, and of this our life, swearing that we
    Are mere usurpers, tyrants, and what's worse,
    To fright the animals, and to kill them up
    In their assign'd and native dwelling-place.

Duke Sr. And did you leave him in this contemplation?
Sec. Lord. We did, my lord, weeping and commenting
   Upon the sobbing deer.
Duke Sr.   Show me the place!
   I love to cope him in these sullen fits,
   For then he's full of matter.
First Lord. I'll bring you to him straight.   *Exeunt*

SCENE II

A room in the palace

Enter Duke Frederick, with Lords

Duke Frederick. Can it be possible that no man saw them?
   It cannot be; some villains of my court
   Are of consent and sufferance in this.
First Lord. I cannot hear of any that did see her;
   The ladies, her attendants of her chamber,
   Saw her a-bed, and in the morning early
   They found the bed untreasur'd of their mistress.
Sec. Lord. My lord, the roynish clown, at whom so oft
   Your Grace was wont to laugh, is also missing;
   Hisperia, the princess' gentlewoman,
   Confesses that she secretly o'erheard
   Your daughter and her cousin much commend
   The parts and graces of the wrestler
   That did but lately foil the sinewy Charles,
   And she believes, wherever they are gone,
   That youth is surely in their company.
Duke Frederick. Send to his brother, fetch that gallant
     hither,
   If he be absent, bring his brother to me,
   I'll make him find him: do this suddenly;
   And let not search and inquisition quail
   To bring again these foolish runaways.   *Exeunt*

SCENE III

Before Oliver's house

Enter Orlando and Adam, meeting

Orlando. Who's there?

Adam. What, my young master? O my gentle master,
    O my sweet master, O you memory
    Of old Sir Rowland! why, what make you here?
    Why are you virtuous? why do people love you?
    And wherefore are you gentle, strong, and valiant?
    Why would you be so fond to overcome
    The bonny priser of the humorous Duke?
    Your praise is come too swiftly home before you.
    Know you not, master, to some kind of men
    Their graces serve them but as enemies?
    No more do yours: your virtues, gentle master,
    Are sanctified and holy traitors to you.
    O, what a world is this, when what is comely
    Envenoms him that bears it!

Orlando. Why, what's the matter?

Adam.   O unhappy youth,
    Come not within these doors: within this roof
    The enemy of all your graces lives,
    Your brother, no, no brother, yet the son
    (Yet not the son, I will not call him son)
    Of him I was about to call his father,
    Hath heard your praises, and this night he means
    To burn the lodging where you use to lie,
    And you within it: if he fail of that,
    He will have other means to cut you off.
    I overheard him; and his practices;
    This is no place, this house is but a butchery:
    Abhor it, fear it, do not enter it.

Orlando. Why, whither, Adam, wouldst thou have me go?
Adam. No matter whither, so you come not here.
Orlando. What, wouldst thou have me go and beg my food?
  Or with a base and boisterous sword enforce
  A thievish living on the common road?
  This I must do, or know not what to do:
  Yet this I will not do, do how I can;
  I rather will subject me to the malice
  Of a diverted blood, and bloody brother.
Adam. But do not so. I have five hundred crowns,
  The thrifty hire I sav'd under your father,
  Which I did store to be my foster-nurse,
  When service should in my old limbs lie lame,
  And unregarded age in corners thrown;
  Take that, and He that doth the ravens feed,
  Yea, providently caters for the sparrow,
  Be comfort to my age! Here is the gold,
  All this I give you, let me be your servant;
  Though I look old, yet I am strong and lusty;
  For in my youth I never did apply
  Hot and rebellious liquors in my blood,
  Nor did not with unbashful forehead woo
  The means of weakness and debility;
  Therefore my age is as a lusty winter,
  Frosty, but kindly: let me go with you,
  I'll do the service of a younger man
  In all your business and necessities.
Orlando. O good old man, how well in thee appears
  The constant service of the antique world,
  When service sweat for duty, not for meed!
  Thou art not for the fashion of these times,
  Where none will sweat, but for promotion,
  And having that do choke their service up,
  Even with the having; it is not so with thee.
  But, poor old man, thou prun'st a rotten tree,
  That cannot so much as a blossom yield,

In lieu of all thy pains and husbandry;
But come thy ways, we'll go along together,
And ere we have thy youthful wages spent,
We'll light upon some settled low content.
Adam. Master, go on, and I will follow thee
To the last gasp, with truth and loyalty;
From seventeen years, till now almost fourscore
Here lived I, but now live here no more.
At seventeen years, many their fortunes seek,
But at fourscore, it is too late a week:
Yet fortune cannot recompense me better
Than to die well, and not my master's debtor.

Exeunt

SCENE IV

The Forest of Arden

*Enter Rosalind for Ganymede, Celia for Aliena,
and Touchstone*

Rosalind. O Jupiter, how weary are my spirits!
Touchstone. I care not for my spirits, if my legs were not
weary.
Rosalind. I could find in my heart to disgrace my man's apparel and to cry like a woman; but I must comfort the
weaker vessel, as doublet and hose ought to show itself
courageous to petticoat; therefore courage, good Aliena.
Celia. I pray you bear with me; I cannot go no further.
Touchstone. For my part, I had rather bear with you than
bear you: yet I should bear no cross if I did bear you, for
I think you have no money in your purse.

Rosalind. Well, this is the forest of Arden.

Touchstone. Ay, now am I in Arden, the more fool I; when
    I was at home I was in a better place, but travellers must
    be content.

Rosalind. Ay, be so, good Touchstone.

Enter Corin and Silvius

Look you, who comes here; a young man and an old in
    solemn talk.

Corin. That is the way to make her scorn you still.

Silvius. O Corin, that thou knew'st how I do love her!

Corin. I partly guess; for I have lov'd ere now.

Silvius. No, Corin, being old, thou canst not guess,
    Though in thy youth thou wast as true a lover
    As ever sigh'd upon a midnight pillow:
    But if thy love were ever like to mine,—
    As sure I think did never man love so,—
    How many actions most ridiculous
    Hast thou been drawn to by thy fantasy?

Corin. Into a thousand that I have forgotten.

Silvius. O, thou didst then ne'er love so heartily,
    If thou remember'st not the slightest folly,
    That ever love did make thee run into,
    Thou hast not lov'd:
    Or if thou hast not sat as I do now,
    Wearing thy hearer in thy mistress' praise,
    Thou hast not lov'd:
    Or if thou hast not broke from company,
    Abruptly as my passion now makes me,
    Thou hast not lov'd.
    O Phebe, Phebe, Phebe!   *Exit*

Rosalind. Alas, poor shepherd! searching of thy wound,
    I have by hard adventure found mine own.

Touchstone. And I mine. I remember when I was in love,
    I broke my sword upon a stone, and bid him take that
    for coming a-night to Jane Smile, and I remember the

kissing of her batler, and the cow's dugs that her pretty
chopt hands had milked: and I remember the wooing of
a peascod instead of her, from whom I took two cods,
and, giving her them again, said with weeping tears 'Wear
these for my sake.' We that are true lovers run into
strange capers; but as all is mortal in nature, so is all
nature in love mortal in folly.

Rosalind. Thou speak'st wiser than thou art ware of.

Touchstone. Nay, I shall ne'er be ware of mine own wit,
till I break my shins against it.

Rosalind. Jove, Jove! this shepherd's passion
Is much upon my fashion.

Touchstone. And mine, but it grows something stale with
me.

Celia. I pray you, one of you question yond man,
If he for gold will give us any food;
I faint almost to death.

Touchstone.   Holla; you clown!

Rosalind. Peace, fool, he's not thy kinsman.

Corin.   Who calls?

Touchstone. Your betters, sir.

Corin.   Else are they very wretched.

Rosalind. Peace, I say. Good even to you, friend.

Corin. And to you, gentle sir, and to you all.

Rosalind. I prithee, shepherd, if that love or gold
Can in this desert place buy entertainment,
Bring us where we may rest ourselves, and feed:
Here's a young maid with travel much oppress'd,
And faints for succour.

Corin.   Fair sir, I pity her,
And wish, for her sake more than for mine own,
My fortunes were more able to relieve her;
But I am shepherd to another man,
And do not shear the fleeces that I graze:
My master is of churlish disposition,
And little recks to find the way to heaven

By doing deeds of hospitality:
Besides, his cote, his flocks, and bounds of feed
Are now on sale, and at our sheepcote now,
By reason of his absence, there is nothing
That you will feed on; but what is, come see,
And in my voice most welcome shall you be.
Rosalind. What is he that shall buy his flock and pasture?
Corin. That young swain that you saw here but erewhile,
  That little cares for buying any thing.
Rosalind. I pray thee, if it stand with honesty,
  Buy thou the cottage, pasture, and the flock,
  And thou shalt have to pay for it of us.
Celia. And we will mend thy wages. I like this place,
  And willingly could waste my time in it.
Corin. Assuredly the thing is to be sold:
  Go with me, if you like upon report
  The soil, the profit, and this kind of life,
  I will your very faithful feeder be,
  And buy it with your gold right suddenly.   *Exeunt*

SCENE V

The Forest of Arden

Enter Amiens, Jaques, and others

SONG

Amiens.   Under the greenwood tree,
                 Who loves to lie with me,
               And turn his merry note,
                 Unto the sweet bird's throat:
           Come hither, come hither, come hither:
                 Here shall he see
                 No enemy,
               But winter and rough weather.

Jaques. More, more, I prithee, more.

Amiens. It will make you melancholy, Monsieur Jaques.

Jaques. I thank it. More, I prithee, more; I can suck melancholy out of a song, as a weasel sucks eggs. More, I prithee, more.

Amiens. My voice is ragged, I know I cannot please you.

Jaques. I do not desire you to please me, I do desire you to sing: come, more, another stanzo: call you 'em stanzos?

Amiens. What you will, Monsieur Jaques.

Jaques. Nay, I care not for their names, they owe me nothing. Will you sing?

Amiens. More at your request than to please myself.

Jaques. Well then, if ever I thank any man, I'll thank you: but that they call compliment is like the encounter of two dog-apes: and when a man thanks me heartily, methinks I have given him a penny, and he renders me the beggarly thanks. Come, sing; and you that will not, hold your tongues.

Amiens. Well, I'll end the song. Sirs, cover the while, the Duke will drink under this tree. He hath been all this day to look you.

Jaques. And I have been all this day to avoid him: he is too disputable for my company: I think of as many matters as he, but I give heaven thanks, and make no boast of them. Come, warble, come.

SONG

Who doth ambition shun, *All together here*
And loves to live i' the sun:
Seeking the food he eats,
And pleased with what he gets:
Come hither, come hither, come hither:
Here shall he see
No enemy,
But winter and rough weather.

Jaques. I'll give you a verse to this note, that I made yesterday in despite of my invention.
Amiens. And I'll sing it.
Jaques. Thus it goes:—

If it do come to pass,
That any man turn ass,
Leaving his wealth and ease,
A stubborn will to please,
Ducdame, ducdame, ducdame:
Here shall he see,
Gross fools as he,
And if he will come to me.

Amiens. What's that 'ducdame'?
Jaques. 'Tis a Greek invocation, to call fools into a circle. I'll go sleep, if I can; if I cannot, I'll rail against all the first-born of Egypt.
Amiens. And I'll go seek the Duke; his banquet is prepared.
                                    Exeunt severally

SCENE VI

The Forest of Arden

Enter Orlando and Adam

Adam. Dear master, I can go no further; O, I die for food!
Here lie I down, and measure out my grave. Farewell,
kind master.

Orlando. Why, how now, Adam? no greater heart in thee?
Live a little, comfort a little, cheer thyself a little. If this
uncouth forest yield any thing savage, I will either be
food for it, or bring it for food to thee: thy conceit is
nearer death than thy powers. For my sake be comfort-
able, hold death awhile at the arm's end: I will here be
with thee presently, and if I bring thee not something
to eat, I will give thee leave to die: but if thou diest before I come, thou art a mocker of my labour. Well said!
thou look'st cheerly, and I'll be with thee quickly: yet
thou liest in the bleak air. Come, I will bear thee to some
shelter, and thou shalt not die for lack of a dinner, if
there live any thing in this desert. Cheerly, good Adam!
Exeunt

SCENE VII

The Forest of Arden

*A table set out. Enter Duke senior, Amiens,
and Lords like outlaws*

Duke Sr. I think he be transform'd into a beast,
For I can no where find him, like a man.
First Lord. My lord, he is but even now gone hence;
Here was he merry, hearing of a song.
Duke Sr. If he, compact of jars, grow musical,

We shall have shortly discord in the spheres.
Go, seek him, tell him I would speak with him.

Enter Jaques

First Lord. He saves my labour by his own approach.
Duke Sr. Why, how now, monsieur? what a life is this,
    That your poor friends must woo your company?
    What, you look merrily!
Jaques. A fool, a fool: I met a fool i' the forest,
    A motley fool; (a miserable world!)
    As I do live by food, I met a fool,
    Who laid him down, and bask'd him in the sun,
    And rail'd on Lady Fortune in good terms,
    In good set terms, and yet a motley fool.
    'Good morrow, fool,' quoth I. 'No, sir,' quoth he,
    'Call me not fool, till heaven hath sent me fortune:'
    And then he drew a dial from his poke,
    And looking on it, with lack-lustre eye,
    Says, very wisely, 'It is ten o'clock:
    Thus we may see,' quoth he, 'how the world wags:
    'Tis but an hour ago since it was nine;
    And after one hour more, 'twill be eleven;
    And so from hour to hour, we ripe, and ripe,
    And then from hour to hour, we rot, and rot,
    And thereby hangs a tale.' When I did hear
    The motley fool thus moral on the time,
    My lungs began to crow like chanticleer,
    That fools should be so deep-contemplative;
    And I did laugh, sans intermission
    An hour by his dial. O noble fool,
    A worthy fool! Motley's the only wear.
Duke Sr. What fool is this?
Jaques. O worthy fool! One that hath been a courtier,
    And says, if ladies be but young, and fair,
    They have the gift to know it: and in his brain,
    Which is as dry as the remainder biscuit

After a voyage, he hath strange places cramm'd
With observation, the which he vents
In mangled forms. O that I were a fool!
I am ambitious for a motley coat.
Duke Sr. Thou shalt have one.
Jaques.   It is my only suit,
Provided that you weed your better judgements
Of all opinion that grows rank in them
That I am wise. I must have liberty
Withal, as large a charter as the wind,
To blow on whom I please, for so fools have;
And they that are most galled with my folly,
They most must laugh. And why, sir, must they so?
The 'why' is plain, as way to parish church:
He that a fool doth very wisely hit
Doth very foolishly, although he smart,
Not to seem senseless of the bob: if not,
The wise man's folly is anatomized
Even by the squandering glances of the fool.
Invest me in my motley; give me leave
To speak my mind, and I will through and through
Cleanse the foul body of the infected world,
If they will patiently receive my medicine.
Duke Sr. Fie on thee! I can tell what thou wouldst do.
Jaques. What, for a counter, would I do but good?
Duke Sr. Most mischievous foul sin, in chiding sin:
For thou thyself hast been a libertine,
As sensual as the brutish sting itself;
And all the embossed sores, and headed evils,
That thou with license of free foot hast caught,
Wouldst thou disgorge into the general world.
Jaques. Why, who cries out on pride,
That can therein tax any private party?
Doth it not flow as hugely as the sea,
Till that the weary very means do ebb?
What woman in the city do I name,

When that I say the city-woman bears
The cost of princes on unworthy shoulders?
Who can come in, and say that I mean her,
When such a one as she, such is her neighbour?
Or what is he of basest function,
That says his bravery is not on my cost,
Thinking that I mean him, but therein suits
His folly to the mettle of my speech?
There then; how then? what then? let me see wherein
My tongue hath wrong'd him: if it do him right,
Then he hath wrong'd himself; if he be free,
Why then my taxing like a wild-goose flies,
Unclaim'd of any man. But who comes here?

Enter Orlando, with his sword drawn

Orlando. Forbear, and eat no more.
Jaques. Why, I have eat none yet.
Orlando. Nor shalt not, till necessity be serv'd.
Jaques. Of what kind should this cock come of?
Duke Sr. Art thou thus bolden'd, man, by thy distress?
Or else a rude despiser of good manners,
That in civility thou seem'st so empty?
Orlando. You touch'd my vein at first, the thorny point
Of bare distress, hath ta'en from me the show
Of smooth civility: yet am I inland bred,
And know some nurture. But forbear, I say,
He dies that touches any of this fruit,
Till I, and my affairs, are answered.
Jaques. An you will not be answer'd with reason, I must
die.
Duke Sr. What would you have? Your gentleness shall force,
More than your force move us to gentleness.
Orlando. I almost die for food, and let me have it.
Duke Sr. Sit down and feed, and welcome to our table.
Orlando. Speak you so gently? Pardon me I pray you,
I thought that all things had been savage here,

And therefore put I on the countenance
Of stern commandment. But whate'er you are
That in this desert inaccessible,
Under the shade of melancholy boughs,
Lose and neglect the creeping hours of time;
If ever you have look'd on better days;
If ever been where bells have knoll'd to church;
If ever sat at any good man's feast;
If ever from your eyelids wip'd a tear,
And know what 'tis to pity, and be pitied;
Let gentleness my strong enforcement be:
In the which hope I blush, and hide my sword.
Duke Sr. True is it, that we have seen better days,
And have with holy bell been knoll'd to church,
And sat at good men's feasts, and wip'd our eyes
Of drops, that sacred pity hath engender'd:
And therefore sit you down in gentleness,
And take upon command what help we have
That to your wanting may be minister'd.
Orlando. Then but forbear your food a little while;
Whiles, like a doe, I go to find my fawn,
And give it food. There is an old poor man,
Who after me hath many a weary step
Limp'd in pure love: till he be first suffic'd,
Oppress'd with two weak evils, age, and hunger,
I will not touch a bit.
Duke Sr.   Go find him out:
And we will nothing waste till you return.
Orlando. I thank ye, and be blest for your good comfort!
                                                        Exit

Duke Sr. Thou seest, we are not all alone unhappy:
This wide and universal theatre
Presents more wooful pageants than the scene
Wherein we play in.
Jaques.   All the world's a stage,
And all the men and women, merely players;

They have their exits and their entrances,
And one man in his time plays many parts,
His acts being seven ages. At first the infant,
Mewling, and puking in the nurse's arms:
Then the whining school-boy with his satchel
And shining morning face, creeping like snail
Unwillingly to school. And then the lover,
Sighing like furnace, with a woeful ballad
Made to his mistress' eyebrow. Then, a soldier,
Full of strange oaths, and bearded like the pard,
Jealous in honour, sudden, and quick in quarrel,
Seeking the bubble reputation
Even in the cannon's mouth: and then, the justice,
In fair round belly, with good capon lin'd,
With eyes severe, and beard of formal cut,
Full of wise saws, and modern instances,
And so he plays his part. The sixth age shifts
Into the lean and slipper'd pantaloon,
With spectacles on nose, and pouch on side,
His youthful hose well sav'd, a world too wide,
For his shrunk shank, and his big manly voice,
Turning again toward childish treble, pipes,
And whistles in his sound. Last scene of all,
That ends this strange eventful history,
Is second childishness, and mere oblivion,
Sans teeth, sans eyes, sans taste, sans every thing.

Re-enter Orlando, with Adam

Duke Sr. Welcome; set down your venerable burthen,
  And let him feed.
Orlando. I thank you most for him.
Adam.   So had you need,
  I scarce can speak to thank you for myself.
Duke Sr. Welcome, fall to: I will not trouble you,
  As yet to question you about your fortunes.
  Give us some music, and, good cousin, sing.

SONG

Amiens.   Blow, blow, thou winter wind,
      Thou art not so unkind,
        As man's ingratitude;
      Thy tooth is not so keen,
      Because thou art not seen,
        Although thy breath be rude.
Heigh-ho! sing, heigh-ho! unto the green holly:
Most friendship is feigning, most loving, mere folly:
      Then, heigh-ho, the holly!
      This life is most jolly.

      Freeze, freeze, thou bitter sky,
      That dost not bite so nigh
        As benefits forgot:
      Though thou the waters warp,
      Thy sting is not so sharp,
        As friend remember'd not.
Heigh-ho! sing, &c.

Duke Sr. If that you were the good Sir Rowland's son,
As you have whisper'd faithfully you were,
And as mine eye doth his effigies witness,
Most truly limn'd, and living in your face,
Be truly welcome hither: I am the Duke
That lov'd your father; the residue of your fortune,
Go to my cave, and tell me. Good old man,
Thou art right welcome, as thy master is.
Support him by the arm. Give me your hand,
And let me all your fortunes understand.　　　*Exeunt*

SCENE I

A room in the palace

Enter Duke Frederick, Lords, and Oliver

Duke Frederick. Not see him since? Sir, sir, that cannot be:
  But were I not the better part made mercy,
  I should not seek an absent argument
  Of my revenge, thou present. But look to it,
  Find out thy brother wheresoe'er he is,
  Seek him with candle; bring him dead, or living,
  Within this twelvemonth, or turn thou no more
  To seek a living in our territory.
  Thy lands and all things that thou dost call thine,
  Worth seizure, do we seize into our hands,
  Till thou canst quit thee by thy brother's mouth,
  Of what we think against thee.
Oliver. O that your Highness knew my heart in this!
  I never lov'd my brother in my life.
Duke Frederick. More villain thou. Well, push him out of
    doors,
  And let my officers of such a nature
  Make an extent upon his house and lands:
  Do this expediently, and turn him going.   *Exeunt*

SCENE II

The forest

Enter Orlando, with a paper

Orlando. Hang there, my verse, in witness of my love,
  And Thou, thrice-crowned queen of night, survey

With thy chaste eye, from thy pale sphere above,
    Thy huntress' name that my full life doth sway.
O Rosalind! these trees shall be my books,
    And in their barks my thoughts I'll character,
That every eye, which in this forest looks,
    Shall see thy virtue witness'd every where.
Run, run, Orlando, carve on every tree,
The fair, the chaste, and unexpressive she.   *Exit*

Enter Corin and Touchstone

Corin. And how like you this shepherd's life, Master Touchstone?

Touchstone. Truly, shepherd, in respect of itself, it is a good life; but in respect that it is a shepherd's life, it is naught. In respect that it is solitary, I like it very well; but in respect that it is private, it is a very vile life. Now, in respect it is in the fields, it pleaseth me well; but in respect it is not in the court, it is tedious. As it is a spare life, look you, it fits my humour well; but as there is no more plenty in it, it goes much against my stomach. Hast any philosophy in thee, shepherd?

Corin. No more but that I know the more one sickens the worse at ease he is; and that he that wants money, means, and content, is without three good friends; that the property of rain is to wet, and fire to burn: that good pasture makes fat sheep: and that a great cause of the night is lack of the sun; that he that hath learned no wit by nature, nor art, may complain of good breeding, or comes of a very dull kindred.

Touchstone. Such a one is a natural philosopher. Wast ever in court, shepherd?

Corin. No, truly.

Touchstone. Then thou art damn'd.

Corin. Nay, I hope.

Touchstone. Truly, thou art damn'd, like an ill-roasted egg, all on one side.

Corin. For not being at court? Your reason.

Touchstone. Why, if thou never wast at court, thou never saw'st good manners: if thou never saw'st good manners, then thy manners must be wicked, and wickedness is sin, and sin is damnation. Thou art in a parlous state, shepherd.

Corin. Not a whit, Touchstone; those that are good manners at the court are as ridiculous in the country as the behaviour of the country is most mockable at the court. You told me, you salute not at the court, but you kiss your hands; that courtesy would be uncleanly if courtiers were shepherds.

Touchstone. Instance, briefly; come, instance.

Corin. Why, we are still handling our ewes, and their fells you know are greasy.

Touchstone. Why, do not your courtier's hands sweat? and is not the grease of a mutton as wholesome as the sweat of a man? Shallow, shallow: a better instance, I say; come.

Corin. Besides, our hands are hard.

Touchstone. Your lips will feel them the sooner. Shallow again: a more sounder instance, come.

Corin. And they are often tarr'd over, with the surgery of our sheep; and would you have us kiss tar? The courtier's hands are perfum'd with civet.

Touchstone. Most shallow man! thou worm's-meat in respect of a good piece of flesh indeed! Learn of the wise and perpend: civet is of a baser birth than tar, the very uncleanly flux of a cat. Mend the instance, shepherd.

Corin. You have too courtly a wit, for me; I'll rest.

Touchstone. Wilt thou rest damn'd? God help thee, shallow man! God make incision in thee! thou art raw.

Corin. Sir, I am a true labourer, I earn that I eat; get that I wear; owe no man hate, envy no man's happiness: glad of other men's good, content with my harm: and the greatest of my pride is to see my ewes graze, and my lambs suck.

Touchstone. That is another simple sin in you, to bring the ewes and the rams together, and to offer to get your liv-

ing by the copulation of cattle, to be bawd to a bell-
wether, and to betray a she-lamb of a twelve-month to a
crooked-pated old cuckoldly ram, out of all reasonable
match. If thou beest not damn'd for this, the devil himself will have no shepherds; I cannot see else how thou
shouldst 'scape.

Corin. Here comes young Master Ganymede, my new mistress's brother.

Enter Rosalind, with a paper, reading

Rosalind.   From the east to western Ind,
        No jewel is like Rosalind;
      Her worth, being mounted on the wind,
        Through all the world bears Rosalind.
      All the pictures fairest lin'd
        Are but black to Rosalind.
      Let no face be kept in mind,
        But the fair of Rosalind.

Touchstone. I'll rhyme you so, eight years together; din-
ners, and suppers, and sleeping-hours excepted: it is the
right butter-women's rank to market.

Rosalind. Out, fool!

Touchstone. For a taste:

      If a hart do lack a hind,
        Let him seek out Rosalind.
      If the cat will after kind,
        So be sure will Rosalind.
      Winter garments must be lin'd,
        So must slender Rosalind.
      They that reap must sheaf and bind,
        Then to cart with Rosalind.
      Sweetest nut hath sourest rind,
        Such a nut is Rosalind.
      He that sweetest rose will find,
        Must find love's prick, and Rosalind.

This is the very false gallop of verses; why do you infect
yourself with them?

Rosalind. Peace, you dull fool! I found them on a tree.

Touchstone. Truly the tree yields bad fruit.

Rosalind. I'll graff it with you, and then I shall graff it with
a medlar: then it will be the earliest fruit i' the country;
for you'll be rotten ere you be half ripe, and that's the
right virtue of the medlar.

Touchstone. You have said; but whether wisely or no, let
the forest judge.

Enter Celia, with a writing

Rosalind. Peace!

Here comes my sister reading: stand aside.

Celia. (*reads*) Why should this desert be,
  For it is unpeopled? No;
 Tongues I'll hang on every tree,
  That shall civil sayings show:
 Some, how brief the life of man
  Runs his erring pilgrimage,
 That the stretching of a span
  Buckles in his sum of age;
 Some, of violated vows,
  'Twixt the souls of friend and friend:
 But upon the fairest boughs,
  Or at every sentence end,
 Will I Rosalinda write,
  Teaching all that read, to know
 The quintessence of every sprite,
  Heaven would in little show.
 Therefore Heaven Nature charg'd
  That one body should be fill'd
 With all graces wide-enlarg'd:
  Nature presently distill'd
 Helen's cheek, but not her heart,
  Cleopatra's majesty,

Atalanta's better part,
　　Sad Lucretia's modesty.
Thus Rosalind of many parts
　　By heavenly synod was devis'd;
Of many faces, eyes, and hearts,
　　To have the touches dearest priz'd.
Heaven would that she these gifts should have,
And I to live and die her slave.

Rosalind. O most gentle pulpiter, what tedious homily of love have you wearied your parishioners withal, and never cried 'Have patience, good people'!

Celia. How now, back-friends? Shepherd, go off a little. Go with him, sirrah.

Touchstone. Come, shepherd, let us make an honourable retreat, though not with bag and baggage, yet with scrip and scrippage.　　　*Exeunt Corin and Touchstone*

Celia. Didst thou hear these verses?

Rosalind. O, yes, I heard them all, and more too, for some of them had in them more feet than the verses would bear.

Celia. That's no matter: the feet might bear the verses.

Rosalind. Ay, but the feet were lame, and could not bear themselves without the verse, and therefore stood lamely in the verse.

Celia. But didst thou hear without wondering how thy name should be hang'd and carved upon these trees?

Rosalind. I was seven of the nine days out of the wonder, before you came: for look here what I found on a palm tree; I was never so be-rhym'd since Pythagoras' time, that I was an Irish rat, which I can hardly remember.

Celia. Trow you who hath done this?

Rosalind. Is it a man?

Celia. And a chain that you once wore about his neck: change you colour?

Rosalind. I prithee, who?

Celia. O Lord, Lord, it is a hard matter for friends to meet;

but mountains may be remov'd with earthquakes, and so
encounter.

Rosalind. Nay, but who is it?

Celia. Is it possible?

Rosalind. Nay, I prithee now, with most petitionary vehe-
mence, tell me who it is.

Celia. O wonderful, wonderful, and most wonderful wonderful, and yet again wonderful, and after that out of all
hooping!

Rosalind. Good my complexion, dost thou think, though I
am caparison'd like a man, I have a doublet and hose
in my disposition? One inch of delay more is a South-sea
of discovery. I prithee, tell me who is it quickly, and
speak apace: I would thou couldst stammer, that thou
might'st pour this conceal'd man out of thy mouth, as
wine comes out of a narrow-mouth'd bottle; either too
much at once, or none at all. I prithee, take the cork out
of thy mouth, that I may drink thy tidings.

Celia. So you may put a man in your belly.

Rosalind. Is he of God's making? What manner of man? Is
his head worth a hat? Or his chin worth a beard?

Celia. Nay, he hath but a little beard.

Rosalind. Why, God will send more, if the man will be
thankful; let me stay the growth of his beard, if thou delay me not the knowledge of his chin.

Celia. It is young Orlando, that tripped up the wrestler's
heels, and your heart, both in an instant.

Rosalind. Nay, but the devil take mocking: speak sad brow,
and true maid.

Celia. I' faith, coz, 'tis he.

Rosalind. Orlando?

Celia. Orlando.

Rosalind. Alas the day, what shall I do with my doublet
and hose? What did he when thou saw'st him? What said
he? How looked he? Wherein went he? What makes he
here? Did he ask for me? Where remains he? How parted

he with thee? and when shalt thou see him again? Answer me in one word.

Celia. You must borrow me Gargantua's mouth first: 'tis a word too great for any mouth of this age's size; to say ay and no, to these particulars, is more than to answer in a catechism.

Rosalind. But doth he know that I am in this forest, and in man's apparel? Looks he as freshly as he did the day he wrestled?

Celia. It is as easy to count atomies as to resolve the propositions of a lover: but take a taste of my finding him, and relish it with good observance. I found him under a tree like a dropped acorn.

Rosalind. It may well be called Jove's tree, when it drops forth such fruit.

Celia. Give me audience, good madam.

Rosalind. Proceed.

Celia. There lay he stretched along like a wounded knight.

Rosalind. Though it be pity to see such a sight, it well becomes the ground.

Celia. Cry 'holla' to thy tongue, I prithee; it curvets unseasonably. He was furnish'd like a hunter.

Rosalind. O ominous, he comes to kill my heart.

Celia. I would sing my song without a burden: thou bring'st me out of tune.

Rosalind. Do you not know I am a woman? when I think, I must speak. Sweet, say on.

Celia. You bring me out. Soft, comes he not here?

Enter Orlando and Jaques

Rosalind. 'Tis he; slink by, and note him.

Jaques. I thank you for your company, but, good faith, I had as lief have been myself alone.

Orlando. And so had I; but yet, for fashion sake,
I thank you too, for your society.

Jaques. Good buy you, let's meet as little as we can.

Orlando. I do desire we may be better strangers.

Jaques. I pray you, mar no more trees with writing love-songs in their barks.

Orlando. I pray you, mar no moe of my verses with reading them ill-favouredly.

Jaques. Rosalind is your love's name?

Orlando. Yes, just.

Jaques. I do not like her name.

Orlando. There was no thought of pleasing you when she was christen'd.

Jaques. What stature is she of?

Orlando. Just as high as my heart.

Jaques. You are full of pretty answers: have you not been acquainted with goldsmiths' wives, and conned them out of rings?

Orlando. Not so; but I answer you right painted cloth, from whence you have studied your questions.

Jaques. You have a nimble wit; I think 'twas made of Atalanta's heels. Will you sit down with me, and we two will rail against our mistress the world, and all our misery.

Orlando. I will chide no breather in the world but myself, against whom I know most faults.

Jaques. The worst fault you have is to be in love.

Orlando. 'Tis a fault I will not change, for your best virtue: I am weary of you.

Jaques. By my troth, I was seeking for a fool, when I found you.

Orlando. He is drown'd in the brook, look but in, and you shall see him.

Jaques. There I shall see mine own figure.

Orlando. Which I take to be either a fool, or a cipher.

Jaques. I'll tarry no longer with you, farewell, good Signior Love.

Orlando. I am glad of your departure: adieu, good Monsieur Melancholy.   *Exit Jaques*

Rosalind. (*aside to Celia*) I will speak to him like a saucy

lackey, and under that habit play the knave with him. Do
you hear, forester?

Orlando. Very well; what would you?

Rosalind. I pray you, what is 't o'clock?

Orlando. You should ask me what time o' day: there's no
clock in the forest.

Rosalind. Then there is no true lover in the forest, else sighing every minute and groaning every hour would detect
the lazy foot of Time as well as a clock.

Orlando. And why not the swift foot of Time? had not that
been as proper?

Rosalind. By no means, sir: Time travels in divers paces,
with divers persons. I'll tell you who Time ambles withal,
who Time trots withal, who Time gallops withal, and
who he stands still withal.

Orlando. I prithee, who doth he trot withal?

Rosalind. Marry, he trots hard with a young maid, between
the contract of her marriage, and the day it is solemniz'd;
if the interim be but a se'nnight, Time's pace is so hard,
that it seems the length of seven year.

Orlando. Who ambles Time withal?

Rosalind. With a priest that lacks Latin, and a rich man that
hath not the gout; for the one sleeps easily because he
cannot study, and the other lives merrily, because he feels
no pain: the one lacking the burden of lean and wasteful
learning; the other knowing no burden of heavy tedious
penury. These Time ambles withal.

Orlando. Who doth he gallop withal?

Rosalind. With a thief to the gallows: for though he go as
softly as foot can fall, he thinks himself too soon there.

Orlando. Who stays it still withal?

Rosalind. With lawyers in the vacation: for they sleep between term and term, and then they perceive not how
Time moves.

Orlando. Where dwell you, pretty youth?

Rosalind. With this shepherdess, my sister; here in the

skirts of the forest, like fringe upon a petticoat.

Orlando. Are you native of this place?

Rosalind. As the cony that you see dwell where she is kindled.

Orlando. Your accent is something finer than you could purchase in so remov'd a dwelling.

Rosalind. I have been told so of many: but indeed, an old religious uncle of mine taught me to speak, who was in his youth an inland man, one that knew courtship too well: for there he fell in love. I have heard him read many lectors against it, and I thank God, I am not a woman to be touch'd with so many giddy offences as he hath generally tax'd their whole sex withal.

Orlando. Can you remember any of the principal evils, that he laid to the charge of women?

Rosalind. There were none principal, they were all like one another, as half-pence are, every one fault seeming monstrous, till his fellow-fault came to match it.

Orlando. I prithee, recount some of them.

Rosalind. No: I will not cast away my physic, but on those that are sick. There is a man haunts the forest, that abuses our young plants with carving Rosalind on their barks; hangs odes upon hawthorns, and elegies on brambles; all, forsooth, defying the name of Rosalind. If I could meet that fancy-monger, I would give him some good counsel, for he seems to have the quotidian of love upon him.

Orlando. I am he that is so love-shak'd, I pray you tell me your remedy.

Rosalind. There is none of my uncle's marks upon you: he taught me how to know a man in love: in which cage of rushes I am sure you are not prisoner.

Orlando. What were his marks?

Rosalind. A lean cheek, which you have not; a blue eye and sunken, which you have not; an unquestionable spirit, which you have not: a beard neglected, which you have not: (but I pardon you for that, for simply your having in beard is a younger brother's revenue): then your hose should be ungarter'd, your bonnet unbanded, your sleeve unbutton'd, your shoe untied, and every thing about you demonstrating a careless desolation: but you are no such man; you are rather point-device in your accoutrements, as loving yourself, than seeming the lover of any other.

Orlando. Fair youth, I would I could make thee believe I love.

Rosalind. Me believe it? You may as soon make her that you love believe it, which I warrant she is apter to do than to confess she does: that is one of the points, in the which women still give the lie to their consciences. But in good sooth, are you he that hangs the verses on the trees, wherein Rosalind is so admir'd?

Orlando. I swear to thee, youth, by the white hand of Rosalind, I am that he, that unfortunate he.

Rosalind. But are you so much in love as your rhymes speak?

Orlando. Neither rhyme nor reason can express how much.

Rosalind. Love is merely a madness, and, I tell you, deserves as well a dark house, and a whip, as madmen do: and the reason why they are not so punish'd and cur'd is, that the lunacy is so ordinary, that the whippers are in love too: yet I profess curing it by counsel.

Orlando. Did you ever cure any so?

Rosalind. Yes, one, and in this manner. He was to imagine me his love, his mistress; and I set him every day to woo me: at which time would I, being but a moonish youth, grieve, be effeminate, changeable, longing, and liking, proud, fantastical, apish, shallow, inconstant, full of tears, full of smiles; for every passion something, and for no passion truly any thing, as boys and women are for the most part cattle of this colour: would now like him, now loathe him; then entertain him, then forswear him; now

weep for him, then spit at him; that I drave my suitor
from his mad humour of love, to a living humour of madness, which was to forswear the full stream of the world,
and to live in a nook merely monastic. And thus I cur'd
him, and this way will I take upon me to wash your liver
as clean as a sound sheep's heart, that there shall not be
one spot of love in 't.

Orlando. I would not be cur'd, youth.

Rosalind. I would cure you, if you would but call me Rosalind and come every day to my cote, and woo me.

Orlando. Now, by the faith of my love, I will; tell me where
it is.

Rosalind. Go with me to it, and I'll show it you: and by the
way you shall tell me where in the forest you live. Will
you go?

Orlando. With all my heart, good youth.

Rosalind. Nay, you must call me Rosalind. Come, sister, will
you go?   *Exeunt*

SCENE III

The forest

Enter Touchstone and Audrey; Jaques behind

Touchstone. Come apace, good Audrey, I will fetch up your
goats, Audrey. And how, Audrey? am I the man yet? doth
my simple feature content you?

Audrey. Your features, Lord warrant us: what features?

Touchstone. I am here with thee, and thy goats, as the most
capricious poet honest Ovid was among the Goths.

Jaques. (*aside*) O knowledge ill-inhabited, worse than
Jove in a thatch'd house!

Touchstone. When a man's verses cannot be understood,

nor a man's good wit seconded with the forward child, understanding, it strikes a man more dead than a great reckoning in a little room. Truly, I would the gods had made thee poetical.

Audrey. I do not know what 'poetical' is: is it honest in deed and word? is it a true thing?

Touchstone. No, truly; for the truest poetry is the most feigning, and lovers are given to poetry: and what they swear in poetry, may be said as lovers, they do feign.

Audrey. Do you wish then that the gods had made me poetical?

Touchstone. I do, truly; for thou swear'st to me thou art honest: now, if thou wert a poet, I might have some hope thou didst feign.

Audrey. Would you not have me honest?

Touchstone. No, truly, unless thou wert hard-favour'd; for honesty coupled to beauty is to have honey a sauce to sugar.

Jaques. (*aside*) A material fool!

Audrey. Well, I am not fair, and therefore I pray the gods make me honest.

Touchstone. Truly, and to cast away honesty upon a foul slut were to put good meat into an unclean dish.

Audrey. I am not a slut, though I thank the gods I am foul.

Touchstone. Well, prais'd be the gods for thy foulness; sluttishness may come hereafter. But be it as it may be, I will marry thee: and to that end, I have been with Sir Oliver Martext, the vicar of the next village, who hath promis'd to meet me in this place of the forest, and to couple us.

Jaques. (*aside*) I would fain see this meeting.

Audrey. Well, the gods give us joy!

Touchstone. Amen. A man may, if he were of a fearful heart, stagger in this attempt; for here we have no temple but the wood, no assembly but horn-beasts. But what though? Courage! As horns are odious, they are neces-

sary. It is said, 'many a man knows no end of his goods:'
right: many a man has good horns, and knows no end of
them. Well, that is the dowry of his wife, 'tis none of his
own getting. Horns?—even so:—poor men alone? No, no,
the noblest deer hath them as huge as the rascal: is the
single man therefore blessed? No, as a wall'd town is
more worthier than a village, so is the forehead of a married man more honourable than the bare brow of a
bachelor: and by how much defence is better than no
skill, by so much is a horn more precious than to want.
Here comes Sir Oliver.

Enter Sir Oliver Martext

Sir Oliver Martext, you are well met. Will you dispatch
us here under this tree, or shall we go with you to your
chapel?

Sir Oliver. Is there none here to give the woman?

Touchstone. I will not take her on gift of any man.

Sir Oliver. Truly, she must be given, or the marriage is not
lawful.

Jaques. Proceed, proceed: I'll give her.

Touchstone. Good even, good Master What-ye-call 't: how
do you, sir? You are very well met: God 'ild you for your
last company, I am very glad to see you, even a toy in
hand here, sir: nay, pray be cover'd.

Jaques. Will you be married, motley?

Touchstone. As the ox hath his bow, sir, the horse his curb,
and the falcon her bells, so man hath his desires, and as
pigeons bill, so wedlock would be nibbling.

Jaques. And will you (being a man of your breeding) be
married under a bush like a beggar? Get you to church,
and have a good priest that can tell you what marriage is;
this fellow will but join you together, as they join wain-
scot; then one of you will prove a shrunk panel, and like
green timber, warp, warp.

Touchstone. (*aside*) I am not in the mind but I were better
   to be married of him than of another, for he is not like
   to marry me well; and not being well married, it will
   be a good excuse for me hereafter, to leave my wife.
Jaques. Go thou with me, and let me counsel thee.
Touchstone. Come, sweet Audrey,
   We must be married, or we must live in bawdry.
   Farewell, good Master Oliver: not,—
                     O sweet Oliver,
                     O brave Oliver,
                  Leave me not behind thee:
but,—
                     Wind away,
                     Begone, I say,
                  I will not to wedding with thee.
                  Exeunt Jaques, Touchstone, and Audrey
Sir Oliver. 'Tis no matter: ne'er a fantastical knave of them
   all shall flout me out of my calling.   *Exit*

SCENE IV

The forest

Enter Rosalind and Celia

Rosalind. Never talk to me, I will weep.

Celia. Do, I prithee, but yet have the grace to consider that tears do not become a man.

Rosalind. But have I not cause to weep?

Celia. As good cause as one would desire, therefore weep.

Rosalind. His very hair is of the dissembling colour.

Celia. Something browner than Judas's: marry, his kisses are Judas's own children.

Rosalind. I' faith, his hair is of a good colour.

Celia. An excellent colour: your chestnut was ever the only colour.

Rosalind. And his kissing is as full of sanctity as the touch of holy bread.

Celia. He hath bought a pair of cast lips of Diana: a nun of winter's sisterhood kisses not more religiously; the very ice of chastity is in them.

Rosalind. But why did he swear he would come this morning, and comes not?

Celia. Nay, certainly, there is no truth in him.

Rosalind. Do you think so?

Celia. Yes, I think he is not a pick-purse, nor a horse-stealer, but for his verity in love, I do think him as concave as a covered goblet, or a worm-eaten nut.

Rosalind. Not true in love?

Celia. Yes, when he is in, but I think he is not in.

Rosalind. You have heard him swear downright he was.

Celia. 'Was' is not 'is': besides, the oath of a lover is no stronger than the word of a tapster, they are both the confirmer of false reckonings; he attends here in the forest on the Duke your father.

Rosalind. I met the Duke yesterday, and had much question
  with him: he ask'd me of what parentage I was; I told
  him, of as good as he, so he laugh'd and let me go. But
  what talk we of fathers, when there is such a man as
  Orlando?

Celia. O, that's a brave man, he writes brave verses, speaks
  brave words, swears brave oaths, and breaks them
  bravely, quite traverse athwart the heart of his lover,
  as a puisny tilter, that spurs his horse but on one side,
  breaks his staff like a noble goose: but all's brave that
  youth mounts, and folly guides. Who comes here?

Enter Corin

Corin. Mistress and master, you have oft inquir'd
  After the shepherd that complain'd of love,
  Who you saw sitting by me on the turf,
  Praising the proud disdainful shepherdess
  That was his mistress.

Celia.   Well; and what of him?

Corin. If you will see a pageant truly play'd
  Between the pale complexion of true love
  And the red glow of scorn and proud disdain,
  Go hence a little, and I shall conduct you
  If you will mark it.

Rosalind.   O, come, let us remove,
  The sight of lovers feedeth those in love:
  Bring us to this sight, and you shall say
  I'll prove a busy actor in their play.   *Exeunt*

SCENE V

The forest

Enter Silvius and Phebe

Silvius. Sweet Phebe, do not scorn me, do not, Phebe;
   Say that you love me not, but say not so
   In bitterness; the common executioner,
   Whose heart the accustom'd sight of death makes hard,
   Falls not the axe upon the humbled neck
   But first begs pardon: will you sterner be
   Than he that dies and lives by bloody drops?

   Enter Rosalind, Celia, and Corin, behind

Phebe. I would not be thy executioner,
   I fly thee, for I would not injure thee:
   Thou tell'st me there is murder in mine eye;
   'Tis pretty, sure, and very probable,
   That eyes, that are the frail'st, and softest things,
   Who shut their coward gates on atomies,
   Should be call'd tyrants, butchers, murderers!
   Now I do frown on thee with all my heart,
   And if mine eyes can wound, now let them kill thee:
   Now counterfeit to swoon, why now fall down,
   Or if thou canst not, O, for shame, for shame,
   Lie not, to say mine eyes are murderers!
   Now show the wound mine eye hath made in thee,
   Scratch thee but with a pin, and there remains
   Some scar of it; lean upon a rush,
   The cicatrice and capable impressure

Thy palm some moment keeps; but now mine eyes,
Which I have darted at thee, hurt thee not,
Nor, I am sure, there is no force in eyes
That can do hurt.

Silvius.　　　　　O dear Phebe,
If ever,—as that ever may be near,—
You meet in some fresh cheek the power of fancy,
Then shall you know the wounds invisible
That Love's keen arrows make.

Phebe.　　　　　　But till that time
Come not thou near me: and when that time comes,
Afflict me with thy mocks, pity me not,
As till that time I shall not pity thee.

Rosalind. And why, I pray you? Who might be your mother,
That you insult, exult, and all at once,
Over the wretched? What though you have no beauty,
As, by my faith, I see no more in you
Than without candle may go dark to bed:
Must you be therefore proud and pitiless?
Why, what means this? Why do you look on me?
I see no more in you than in the ordinary
Of nature's sale-work. 'Od's my little life,
I think she means to tangle my eyes too:
No, faith, proud mistress, hope not after it,
'Tis not your inky brows, your black silk hair,
Your bugle eyeballs, nor your cheek of cream,
That can entame my spirits to your worship:
You foolish shepherd, wherefore do you follow her
Like foggy south, puffing with wind and rain?
You are a thousand times a properer man
Than she a woman. 'Tis such fools as you
That makes the world full of ill-favour'd children:
'Tis not her glass, but you, that flatters her,
And out of you she sees herself more proper
Than any of her lineaments can show her:
But, mistress, know yourself, down on your knees,

And thank heaven, fasting, for a good man's love;
For I must tell you friendly in your ear,
Sell when you can, you are not for all markets:
Cry the man mercy, love him, take his offer,
Foul is most foul, being foul to be a scoffer.
So take her to thee, shepherd: fare you well.

Phebe. Sweet youth, I pray you, chide a year together,
I had rather hear you chide than this man woo.

Rosalind. He's fall'n in love with your foulness, and she'll
fall in love with my anger. If it be so, as fast as she
answers thee with frowning looks, I'll sauce her with bitter words. Why look you so upon me?

Phebe. For no ill will I bear you.

Rosalind. I pray you do not fall in love with me,
For I am falser than vows made in wine:
Besides, I like you not: if you will know my house,
'Tis at the tuft of olives, here hard by.
Will you go, sister? Shepherd, ply her hard.
Come, sister. Shepherdess, look on him better,
And be not proud, though all the world could see,
None could be so abus'd in sight as he.
Come, to our flock.   *Exeunt Rosalind, Celia and Corin*

Phebe. Dead shepherd, now I find thy saw of might,
'Who ever lov'd, that lov'd not at first sight?'

Silvius. Sweet Phebe,—

Phebe.   Ha; what say'st thou, Silvius?

Silvius. Sweet Phebe, pity me.

Phebe. Why, I am sorry for thee, gentle Silvius.

Silvius. Wherever sorrow is, relief would be:
If you do sorrow at my grief in love,
By giving love, your sorrow, and my grief,
Were both extermin'd.

Phebe. Thou hast my love, is not that neighbourly?

Silvius. I would have you.

Phebe.   Why, that were covetousness.
Silvius, the time was that I hated thee;

And yet it is not that I bear thee love,
But since that thou canst talk of love so well,
Thy company, which erst was irksome to me,
I will endure; and I'll employ thee too:
But do not look for further recompense
Than thine own gladness, that thou art employ'd.
Silvius. So holy, and so perfect is my love,
And I in such a poverty of grace,
That I shall think it a most plenteous crop
To glean the broken ears after the man
That the main harvest reaps: loose now and then
A scatter'd smile, and that I'll live upon.
Phebe. Know'st thou the youth that spoke to me erewhile?
Silvius. Not very well, but I have met him oft,
And he hath bought the cottage and the bounds
That the old carlot once was master of.
Phebe. Think not I love him, though I ask for him;
'Tis but a peevish boy, yet he talks well;
But what care I for words? yet words do well
When he that speaks them pleases those that hear:
It is a pretty youth, not very pretty,
But, sure, he's proud, and yet his pride becomes him;
He'll make a proper man: the best thing in him
Is his complexion: and faster than his tongue
Did make offence, his eye did heal it up:
He is not very tall, yet for his years he's tall:
His leg is but so so, and yet 'tis well:
There was a pretty redness in his lip,
A little riper, and more lusty red
Than that mix'd in his cheek; 'twas just the difference
Betwixt the constant red and mingled damask.
There be some women, Silvius, had they mark'd him
In parcels as I did, would have gone near
To fall in love with him: but, for my part,
I love him not, nor hate him not; and yet
I have more cause to hate him than to love him,

For what had he to do to chide at me?
He said mine eyes were black, and my hair black,
And, now I am remember'd, scorn'd at me:
I marvel why I answer'd not again,
But that's all one: omittance is no quittance:
I'll write to him a very taunting letter,
And thou shalt bear it, wilt thou, Silvius?

Silvius. Phebe, with all my heart.

Phebe.   I'll write it straight;
The matter's in my head, and in my heart,
I will be bitter with him, and passing short;
Go with me, Silvius.   *Exeunt*

ACT IV

SCENE 1

The forest

Enter Rosalind, Celia, and Jaques

Jaques. I prithee, pretty youth, let me be better acquainted with thee.

Rosalind. They say you are a melancholy fellow.

Jaques. I am so; I do love it better than laughing.

Rosalind. Those that are in extremity of either are abominable fellows, and betray themselves to every modern censure, worse than drunkards.

Jaques. Why, 'tis good to be sad and say nothing.

Rosalind. Why then, 'tis good to be a post.

Jaques. I have neither the scholar's melancholy, which is emulation; nor the musician's, which is fantastical; nor the courtier's, which is proud; nor the soldier's, which is ambitious; nor the lawyer's, which is politic; nor the lady's, which is nice; nor the lover's, which is all these: but it is a melancholy of mine own, compounded of many simples, extracted from many objects, and indeed the sundry contemplation of my travels, in which by often rumination wraps me in a most humorous sadness.

Rosalind. A traveller! By my faith, you have great reason to be sad: I fear you have sold your own lands, to see other men's; then, to have seen much, and to have nothing, is to have rich eyes, and poor hands.

Jaques. Yes, I have gain'd my experience.

Rosalind. And your experience makes you sad: I had rather have a fool to make me merry than experience to make me sad, and to travel for it too!

Enter Orlando

Orlando. Good-day, and happiness, dear Rosalind!

Jaques. Nay, then, God buy you, an you talk in blank verse.

Rosalind. Farewell, Monsieur Traveller: look you lisp, and wear strange suits; disable all the benefits of your own country; be out of love with your nativity, and almost chide God for making you that countenance you are; or I will scarce think you have swam in a gondola. (*exit Jaques.*) Why, how now, Orlando, where have you been all this while? You a lover! An you serve me such another trick, never come in my sight more.

Orlando. My fair Rosalind, I come within an hour of my promise.

Rosalind. Break an hour's promise in love! He that will divide a minute into a thousand parts, and break but a part of the thousandth part of a minute in the affairs of love, it may be said of him that Cupid hath clapped him o' the shoulder, but I'll warrant him heart-whole.

Orlando. Pardon me, dear Rosalind.

Rosalind. Nay, an you be so tardy, come no more in my sight, I had as lief be woo'd of a snail.

Orlando. Of a snail?

Rosalind. Ay, of a snail: for though he comes slowly, he carries his house on his head; a better jointure, I think, than you make a woman: besides, he brings his destiny with him.

Orlando. What's that?

Rosalind. Why, horns: which such as you are fain to be beholding to your wives for: but he comes armed in his fortune, and prevents the slander of his wife.

Orlando. Virtue is no horn-maker: and my Rosalind is virtuous.

Rosalind. And I am your Rosalind.

Celia. It pleases him to call you so; but he hath a Rosalind of a better leer than you.

Rosalind. Come, woo me, woo me: for now I am in a holiday humour, and like enough to consent. What would you say to me now, an I were your very, very Rosalind?

Orlando. I would kiss before I spoke.

Rosalind. Nay, you were better speak first, and when you were gravell'd, for lack of matter, you might take occasion to kiss: very good orators, when they are out, they will spit, and for lovers, lacking (God warrant us!) matter, the cleanliest shift is to kiss.

Orlando. How if the kiss be denied?

Rosalind. Then she puts you to entreaty, and there begins new matter.

Orlando. Who could be out, being before his beloved mistress?

Rosalind. Marry, that should you, if I were your mistress, or I should think my honesty ranker than my wit.

Orlando. What, of my suit?

Rosalind. Not out of your apparel, and yet out of your suit. Am not I your Rosalind?

Orlando. I take some joy to say you are, because I would be talking of her.

Rosalind. Well, in her person, I say I will not have you.

Orlando. Then in mine own person, I die.

Rosalind. No, faith, die by attorney: the poor world is almost six thousand years old, and in all this time there was not any man died in his own person, videlicet, in a love-cause: Troilus had his brains dash'd out with a Grecian club, yet he did what he could to die before, and he is one of the patterns of love. Leander, he would have liv'd many a fair year though Hero had turn'd nun; if it had not been for a hot midsummer night, for, good youth, he went but forth to wash him in the Hellespont, and being taken with the cramp, was drown'd, and the foolish chroniclers of that age found it was 'Hero of Sestos.' But these are all lies, men have died from time to time, and worms have eaten them, but not for love.

Orlando. I would not have my right Rosalind of this mind, for I protest her frown might kill me.

Rosalind. By this hand, it will not kill a fly. But come, now I will be your Rosalind in a more coming-on disposition: and ask me what you will, I will grant it.

Orlando. Then love me, Rosalind.

Rosalind. Yes, faith, will I, Fridays and Saturdays, and all.

Orlando. And wilt thou have me?

Rosalind. Ay, and twenty such.

Orlando. What sayest thou?

Rosalind. Are you not good?

Orlando. I hope so.

Rosalind. Why then, can one desire too much of a good thing? Come, sister, you shall be the priest, and marry us: give me your hand, Orlando. What do you say, sister?

Orlando. Pray thee, marry us.

Celia. I cannot say the words.

Rosalind. You must begin, 'Will you, Orlando—'

Celia. Go to. Will you, Orlando, have to wife this Rosalind?

Orlando. I will.

Rosalind. Ay, but when?

Orlando. Why now, as fast as she can marry us.

Rosalind. Then you must say 'I take thee, Rosalind, for wife.'

Orlando. I take thee, Rosalind, for wife.

Rosalind. I might ask you for your commission, but I do take thee, Orlando, for my husband: there's a girl goes before the priest, and certainly a woman's thought runs before her actions.

Orlando. So do all thoughts, they are wing'd.

Rosalind. Now tell me how long you would have her, after you have possess'd her.

Orlando. For ever, and a day.

Rosalind. Say 'a day,' without the 'ever.' No, no, Orlando, men are April when they woo, December when they wed: maids are May when they are maids, but the sky changes when they are wives. I will be more jealous of thee than a Barbary cock-pigeon over his hen, more clamorous than a parrot against rain, more new-fangled than an ape, more giddy in my desires than a monkey: I will weep for nothing, like Diana in the fountain, and I will do that when you are dispos'd to be merry; I will laugh like a hyen, and that when thou art inclin'd to sleep.

Orlando. But will my Rosalind do so?

Rosalind. By my life, she will do as I do.

Orlando. O, but she is wise.

Rosalind. Or else she could not have the wit to do this: the wiser, the waywarder: make the doors upon a woman's wit, and it will out at the casement: shut that, and 'twill out at the key-hole: stop that, 'twill fly with the smoke out at the chimney.

Orlando. A man that had a wife with such a wit, he might say 'Wit, whither wilt?'

Rosalind. Nay, you might keep that check for it, till you met your wife's wit going to your neighbour's bed.

Orlando. And what wit could wit have, to excuse that.

Rosalind. Marry, to say she came to seek you there: you shall never take her without her answer, unless you take her without her tongue. O, that woman that cannot make her fault her husband's occasion, let her never nurse her child herself, for she will breed it like a fool!

Orlando. For these two hours, Rosalind, I will leave thee.

Rosalind. Alas, dear love, I cannot lack thee two hours.

Orlando. I must attend the Duke at dinner, by two o'clock I will be with thee again.

Rosalind. Ay, go your ways, go your ways: I knew what you would prove, my friends told me as much, and I thought no less: that flattering tongue of yours won me: 'tis but one cast away, and so, come, death! Two o'clock is your hour?

Orlando. Ay, sweet Rosalind.

Rosalind. By my troth, and in good earnest, and so God mend me, and by all pretty oaths that are not dangerous, if you break one jot of your promise, or come one min-

ute behind your hour, I will think you the most patheti-
cal break-promise, and the most hollow lover, and the
most unworthy of her you call Rosalind, that may be
chosen out of the gross band of the unfaithful: therefore
beware my censure, and keep your promise.

Orlando. With no less religion than if thou wert indeed my
Rosalind: so adieu.

Rosalind. Well, Time is the old justice that examines all such
offenders, and let Time try: adieu.   *Exit Orlando*

Celia. You have simply misus'd our sex in your loveprate:
we must have your doublet and hose pluck'd over your
head, and show the world what the bird hath done to
her own nest.

Rosalind. O coz, coz, coz: my pretty little coz, that thou
didst know how many fathom deep I am in love! But it
cannot be sounded: my affection hath an unknown bottom, like the bay of Portugal.

Celia. Or rather, bottomless, that as fast as you pour affection in, it runs out.

Rosalind. No, that same wicked bastard of Venus, that
was begot of thought, conceiv'd of spleen, and born of
madness, that blind rascally boy, that abuses every one's
eyes because his own are out, let him be judge, how deep
I am in love: I'll tell thee, Aliena, I cannot be out of the
sight of Orlando: I'll go find a shadow, and sigh till he
come.

Celia. And I'll sleep.   *Exeunt*

SCENE II

The forest

Enter Jaques and Lords, foresters

Jaques. Which is he that killed the deer?

A Lord. Sir, it was I.

Jaques. Let's present him to the Duke like a Roman conqueror, and it would do well to set the deer's horns upon his head, for a branch of victory; have you no song, forester, for this purpose?

A Lord. Yes, sir.

Jaques. Sing it: 'tis no matter how it be in tune, so it make noise enough.

SONG

What shall he have that kill'd the deer?
His leather skin, and horns to wear:
Then sing him home: the rest shall bear
    This burden.
Take thou no scorn to wear the horn,
It was a crest ere thou wast born,
    Thy father's father wore it,
    And thy father bore it:
The horn, the horn, the lusty horn,
Is not a thing to laugh to scorn.   *Exeunt*

SCENE III

Enter Rosalind and Celia

Rosalind. How say you now, is it not past two o'clock? and
here much Orlando!

Celia. I warrant you, with pure love, and troubled brain,
he hath ta'en his bow and arrows, and is gone forth to
sleep: look, who comes here.

Enter Silvius

Silvius. My errand is to you, fair youth;
My gentle Phebe did bid me give you this:
I know not the contents, but, as I guess
By the stern brow, and waspish action
Which she did use, as she was writing of it,
It bears an angry tenour; pardon me,
I am but as a guiltless messenger.

Rosalind. Patience herself would startle at this letter,
And play the swaggerer; bear this, bear all:
She says I am not fair, that I lack manners,
She calls me proud, and that she could not love me
Were man as rare as phœnix: 'od's my will,
Her love is not the hare that I do hunt,
Why writes she so to me? Well, shepherd, well,
This is a letter of your own device.

Silvius. No, I protest, I know not the contents.
Phebe did write it.

Rosalind.   Come, come, you are a fool,
And turn'd into the extremity of love.
I saw her hand, she has a leathern hand,
A freestone-colour'd hand, I verily did think
That her old gloves were on, but 'twas her hands:
She has a huswife's hand, but that's no matter:
I say she never did invent this letter,

This is a man's invention, and his hand.

Silvius. Sure, it is hers.

Rosalind. Why, 'tis a boisterous and a cruel style,
A style for challengers: why, she defies me,
Like Turk to Christian: women's gentle brain
Could not drop forth such giant rude invention,
Such Ethiop words, blacker in their effect
Than in their countenance. Will you hear the letter?

Silvius. So please you, for I never heard it yet;
Yet heard too much of Phebe's cruelty.

Rosalind. She Phebes me: mark how the tyrant writes.
(*reads*) Art thou god to shepherd turn'd,
   That a maiden's heart hath burn'd?
Can a woman rail thus?

Silvius. Call you this railing?

Rosalind. (*reads*)
   Why, thy godhead laid apart,
   Warr'st thou with a woman's heart?
Did you ever hear such railing?
   Whiles the eye of man did woo me,
   That could do no vengeance to me.
Meaning me a beast.
   If the scorn of your bright eyne
   Have power to raise such love in mine,
   Alack, in me, what strange effect
   Would they work in mild aspect?
   Whiles you chid me, I did love,
   How then might your prayers move?
   He that brings this love to thee,
   Little knows this love in me:
   And by him seal up thy mind,
   Whether that thy youth and kind
   Will the faithful offer take
   Of me, and all that I can make,
   Or else by him my love deny,
   And then I'll study how to die.

Silvius. Call you this chiding?

Celia. Alas, poor shepherd!

Rosalind. Do you pity him? no, he deserves no pity: wilt
thou love such a woman? What, to make thee an instru-
ment, and play false strains upon thee? not to be endur'd!
Well, go your way to her; (for I see love hath made thee
a tame snake) and say this to her; that if she love me,
I charge her to love thee: if she will not, I will never have
her, unless thou entreat for her: if you be a true lover,
hence, and not a word; for here comes more com-
pany.   *Exit Silvius*

Enter Oliver

Oliver. Good morrow, fair ones: pray you, if you know,
  Where in the purlieus of this forest stands
  A sheep-cote, fenc'd about with olive-trees?

Celia. West of this place, down in the neighbour bottom,
  The rank of osiers, by the murmuring stream
  Left on your right hand, brings you to the place:
  But at this hour the house doth keep itself,
  There's none within.

Oliver. If that an eye may profit by a tongue,
  Then should I know you by description,
  Such garments, and such years: 'The boy is fair,
  Of female favour, and bestows himself
  Like a ripe forester: the woman low
  And browner than her brother': are not you
  The owner of the house I did enquire for?

Celia. It is no boast, being ask'd, to say we are.

Oliver. Orlando doth commend him to you both,
  And to that youth he calls his Rosalind
  He sends this bloody napkin; are you he?

Rosalind. I am: what must we understand by this?

Oliver. Some of my shame, if you will know of me
  What man I am, and how, and why, and where
  This handkercher was stain'd.

Celia.   I pray you tell it.
Oliver. When last the young Orlando parted from you,
    He left a promise to return again
    Within an hour, and pacing through the forest,
    Chewing the food of sweet and bitter fancy,
    Lo, what befel! he threw his eye aside,
    And mark what object did present itself
    Under an old oak, whose boughs were moss'd with age
    And high top, bald with dry antiquity:
    A wretched ragged man, o'ergrown with hair,
    Lay sleeping on his back; about his neck
    A green and gilded snake had wreath'd itself,
    Who with her head nimble in threats approach'd
    The opening of his mouth: but suddenly
    Seeing Orlando, it unlink'd itself,
    And with indented glides did slip away
    Into a bush, under which bush's shade
    A lioness, with udders all drawn dry,
    Lay couching head on ground, with catlike watch
    When that the sleeping man should stir; for 'tis
    The royal disposition of that beast
    To prey on nothing that doth seem as dead:
    This seen, Orlando did approach the man,
    And found it was his brother, his elder brother.
Celia. O, I have heard him speak of that same brother;
    And he did render him the most unnatural
    That liv'd amongst men.
Oliver.   And well he might so do,
    For well I know he was unnatural.
Rosalind. But to Orlando: did he leave him there,
    Food to the suck'd and hungry lioness?
Oliver. Twice did he turn his back, and purpos'd so:
    But kindness, nobler ever than revenge,
    And nature stronger than his just occasion,
    Made him give battle to the lioness:
    Who quickly fell before him, in which hurtling

From miserable slumber I awak'd.
Celia. Are you his brother?
Rosalind.   Was 't you he rescu'd?
Celia. Was 't you that did so oft contrive to kill him?
Oliver. 'Twas I: but 'tis not I: I do not shame
  To tell you what I was, since my conversion
  So sweetly tastes, being the thing I am.
Rosalind. But for the bloody napkin?
Oliver.   By and by:
  When from the first to last betwixt us two
  Tears our recountments had most kindly bath'd,
  As how I came into that desert place;
  In brief, he led me to the gentle Duke,
  Who gave me fresh array, and entertainment,
  Committing me unto my brother's love,
  Who led me instantly unto his cave,
  There stripp'd himself, and here upon his arm
  The lioness had torn some flesh away,
  Which all this while had bled; and now he fainted,
  And cried in fainting upon Rosalind.
  Brief, I recover'd him, bound up his wound,
  And after some small space, being strong at heart,
  He sent me hither, stranger as I am,
  To tell this story, that you might excuse
  His broken promise, and to give this napkin
  Dyed in his blood, unto the shepherd youth,
  That he in sport doth call his Rosalind.   *Rosalind swoons*
Celia. Why, how now, Ganymede, sweet Ganymede?
Oliver. Many will swoon when they do look on blood.
Celia. There is more in it; cousin—Ganymede!
Oliver. Look, he recovers.
Rosalind. I would I were at home.
Celia.   We'll lead you thither.
  I pray you, will you take him by the arm?
Oliver. Be of good cheer, youth: you a man? you lack a
  man's heart.

Rosalind. I do so, I confess it. Ah, sirrah, a body would think this was well counterfeited, I pray you, tell your brother how well I counterfeited. Heigh-ho!

Oliver. This was not counterfeit, there is too great testimony in your complexion that it was a passion of earnest.

Rosalind. Counterfeit, I assure you.

Oliver. Well then, take a good heart, and counterfeit to be a man.

Rosalind. So I do: but, i' faith, I should have been a woman by right.

Celia. Come, you look paler and paler: pray you, draw homewards: good sir, go with us.

Oliver. That will I: for I must bear answer back
How you excuse my brother, Rosalind.

Rosalind. I shall devise something: but I pray you commend my counterfeiting to him. Will you go?   *Exeunt*

ACT V

SCENE 1

The forest

Enter Touchstone and Audrey

Touchstone. We shall find a time, Audrey; patience, gentle Audrey.

Audrey. Faith, the priest was good enough, for all the old gentleman's saying.

Touchstone. A most wicked Sir Oliver, Audrey, a most vile Martext. But Audrey, there is a youth here in the forest lays claim to you.

Audrey. Ay, I know who 'tis: he hath no interest in me in the world: here comes the man you mean.

Touchstone. It is meat and drink to me to see a clown: by my troth, we that have good wits have much to answer for; we shall be flouting; we cannot hold.

Enter William

William. Good ev'n, Audrey.

Audrey. God ye good ev'n, William.

William. And good ev'n to you, sir.

Touchstone. Good ev'n, gentle friend. Cover thy head, cover thy head; nay, prithee, be cover'd. How old are you, friend?

William. Five and twenty, sir.

Touchstone. A ripe age: is thy name William?

William. William, sir.

Touchstone. A fair name. Wast born i' the forest here?

William. Ay, sir, I thank God.

Touchstone. 'Thank God;' a good answer. Art rich?

William. Faith, sir, so so.

Touchstone. 'So so' is good, very good, very excellent good; and yet it is not, it is but so so. Art thou wise?

William. Ay, sir, I have a pretty wit.

Touchstone. Why, thou say'st well. I do now remember a saying, 'The fool doth think he is wise, but the wise man knows himself to be a fool.' The heathen philosopher, when he had a desire to eat a grape, would open his lips when he put it into his mouth, meaning thereby, that grapes were made to eat, and lips to open. You do love this maid?

William. I do, sir.

Touchstone. Give me your hand. Art thou learned?

William. No, sir.

Touchstone. Then learn this of me: to have, is to have. For it is a figure in rhetoric, that drink being pour'd out of a cup into a glass, by filling the one, doth empty the other. For all your writers do consent, that *ipse* is he: now you are not *ipse*, for I am he.

William. Which he, sir?

Touchstone. He, sir, that must marry this woman: therefore, you clown, abandon,—which is in the vulgar leave —the society,—which in the boorish is company,—of this female,—which in the common is woman: which together, is, abandon the society of this female, or, clown, thou perishest: or, to thy better understanding, diest; or, to wit, I kill thee, make thee away, translate thy life into death, thy liberty into bondage: I will deal in poison with thee, or in bastinado, or in steel: I will bandy with thee in faction, I will o'er-run thee with policy; I will kill thee a hundred and fifty ways, therefore tremble, and depart.

Audrey. Do, good William.

William. God rest you merry, sir.   *Exit*

Enter Corin

Corin. Our master and mistress seeks you; come away, away!

Touchstone. Trip, Audrey! trip, Audrey! I attend, I attend.
Exeunt

SCENE II

The forest

Enter Orlando and Oliver

Orlando. Is 't possible that on so little acquaintance you
should like her? that, but seeing, you should love her?
and loving woo? and wooing, she should grant? and will
you persever to enjoy her?

Oliver. Neither call the giddiness of it in question; the poverty of her, the small acquaintance, my sudden wooing,
nor sudden consenting: but say with me, I love Aliena;
say with her, that she loves me; consent with both, that
we may enjoy each other: it shall be to your good; for
my father's house, and all the revenue that was old Sir
Rowland's, will I estate upon you, and here live and die
a shepherd.

Orlando. You have my consent. Let your wedding be to-
morrow: thither will I invite the Duke, and all 's con-
tented followers. Go you, and prepare Aliena; for look
you, here comes my Rosalind.

Enter Rosalind

Rosalind. God save you, brother.

Oliver. And you, fair sister.   *Exit*

Rosalind. O, my dear Orlando, how it grieves me to see
thee wear thy heart in a scarf!

Orlando. It is my arm.

Rosalind. I thought thy heart had been wounded with the
claws of a lion.

Orlando. Wounded it is, but with the eyes of a lady.

Rosalind. Did your brother tell you how I counterfeited to
swoon, when he show'd me your handkercher?

Orlando. Ay, and greater wonders than that.

Rosalind. O, I know where you are: nay, 'tis true: there
was never any thing so sudden, but the fight of two rams,
and Cæsar's thrasonical brag of 'I came, saw, and over-
came:' for your brother, and my sister, no sooner met, but
they look'd; no sooner look'd, but they lov'd; no sooner
lov'd, but they sigh'd; no sooner sigh'd but they ask'd
one another the reason; no sooner knew the reason, but
they sought the remedy: and in these degrees, have they
made a pair of stairs to marriage, which they will climb
incontinent, or else be incontinent before marriage: they
are in the very wrath of love and they will together.
Clubs cannot part them.

Orlando. They shall be married to-morrow: and I will bid
the Duke to the nuptial. But, O, how bitter a thing it is,
to look into happiness through another man's eyes! By
so much the more shall I to-morrow be at the height of
heart-heaviness, by how much I shall think my brother
happy, in having what he wishes for.

Rosalind. Why, then, to-morrow I cannot serve your turn
for Rosalind?

Orlando. I can live no longer by thinking.

Rosalind. I will weary you then no longer with idle talking.
Know of me then (for now I speak to some purpose)
that I know you are a gentleman of good conceit: I
speak not this that you should bear a good opinion of
my knowledge: insomuch (I say) I know you are; neither
do I labour for a greater esteem than may in some little
measure draw a belief from you, to do yourself good,
and not to grace me. Believe then, if you please, that I
can do strange things: I have, since I was three year old,
convers'd with a magician, most profound in his art, and
yet not damnable. If you do love Rosalind so near the
heart as your gesture cries it out: when your brother mar-
ries Aliena, shall you marry her. I know into what straits
of fortune she is driven, and it is not impossible to me,

if it appear not inconvenient to you, to set her before
your eyes to-morrow, human as she is, and without any
danger.

Orlando. Speak'st thou in sober meanings?

Rosalind. By my life, I do, which I tender dearly, though
I say I am a magician. Therefore put you in your best
array, bid your friends; for if you will be married to-
morrow, you shall; and to Rosalind, if you will.

Enter Silvius and Phebe

Look, here comes a lover of mine, and a lover of hers.

Phebe. Youth, you have done me much ungentleness,
To show the letter that I writ to you.

Rosalind. I care not if I have: it is my study
To seem despiteful and ungentle to you:
You are there followed by a faithful shepherd,
Look upon him, love him; he worships you.

Phebe. Good shepherd, tell this youth what 'tis to love.

Silvius. It is to be all made of sighs and tears,
And so am I for Phebe.

Phebe. And I for Ganymede.

Orlando. And I for Rosalind.

Rosalind. And I for no woman.

Silvius. It is to be all made of faith and service,
And so am I for Phebe.

Phebe. And I for Ganymede.

Orlando. And I for Rosalind.

Rosalind. And I for no woman.

Silvius. It is to be all made of fantasy,
All made of passion, and all made of wishes,
All adoration, duty, and observance,
All humbleness, all patience, and impatience,
All purity, all trial, all observance;
And so am I for Phebe.

Phebe. And so am I for Ganymede.

Orlando. And so am I for Rosalind.

Rosalind. And so am I for no woman.

Phebe. If this be so, why blame you me to love you?

Silvius. If this be so, why blame you me to love you?

Orlando. If this be so, why blame you me to love you?

Rosalind. Who do you speak to, 'Why blame you me to love you?'

Orlando. To her that is not here, nor doth not hear.

Rosalind. Pray you, no more of this, 'tis like the howling of Irish wolves against the moon. (*To Silvius*) I will help you, if I can: (*To Phebe*) I would love you, if I could. To-morrow meet me all together. (*To Phebe*) I will marry you, if ever I marry woman, and I'll be married to-morrow: (*To Orlando*) I will satisfy you, if ever I satisfied man, and you shall be married to-morrow: (*To Silvius*) I will content you, of what pleases you contents you, and you shall be married to-morrow. (*To Orlando*) As you love Rosalind, meet: (*To Silvius*) as you love Phebe, meet: and as I love no woman, I'll meet. So, fare you well: I have left you commands.

Silvius. I'll not fail, if I live.

Phebe. Nor I.

Orlando. Nor I.   *Exeunt*

SCENE III

The forest

Enter Touchstone and Audrey

Touchstone. To-morrow is the joyful day, Audrey, to-morrow will we be married.

Audrey. I do desire it with all my heart; and I hope it is no dishonest desire, to desire to be a woman of the world? Here come two of the banish'd Duke's pages.

Enter two Pages

First Page. Well met, honest gentleman.

Touchstone. By my troth, well met: come, sit, sit, and a song.

Sec. Page. We are for you, sit i' the middle.

First Page. Shall we clap into 't roundly, without hawking, or spitting, or saying we are hoarse, which are the only prologues to a bad voice?

Sec. Page. I' faith, i' faith, and both in a tune like two gipsies on a horse.

SONG

It was a lover, and his lass,
   With a hey, and a ho, and a hey nonino,
That o'er the green corn-field did pass,
   In the spring time, the only pretty ring time,
When birds do sing, hey ding a ding, ding:
   Sweet lovers love the spring.

Between the acres of the rye,
  With a hey, and a ho, and a hey nonino,
These pretty country folks would lie,
  In spring time, &c.

This carol they began that hour,
  With a hey, and a ho, and a hey nonino,
How that a life was but a flower
  In spring time, &c.

And therefore take the present time,
  With a hey, and a ho, and a hey nonino;
For love is crowned with the prime
  In spring time, &c.

Touchstone. Truly, young gentlemen, though there was no
  great matter in the ditty, yet the note was very untune-
  able.
First Page. You are deceiv'd, sir, we kept time, we lost not
  our time.
Touchstone. By my troth, yes; I count it but time lost to
  hear such a foolish song. God buy you, and God mend
  your voices! Come, Audrey.   *Exeunt*

SCENE IV

The forest

*Enter Duke senior, Amiens, Jaques, Orlando,
Oliver, and Celia*

Duke Sr. Dost thou believe, Orlando, that the boy
  Can do all this that he hath promised?
Orlando. I sometimes do believe, and sometimes do not,
  As those that fear they hope, and know they fear.

Enter Rosalind, Silvius, and Phebe

Rosalind. Patience once more, whiles our compact is urg'd:
  You say, if I bring in your Rosalind,
  You will bestow her on Orlando here?

Duke Sr. That would I, had I kingdoms to give with her.

Rosalind. And you say you will have her, when I bring her.

Orlando. That would I, were I of all kingdoms king.

Rosalind. You say, you'll marry me, if I be willing?

Phebe. That will I, should I die the hour after.

Rosalind. But if you do refuse to marry me,
  You'll give yourself to this most faithful shepherd?

Phebe. So is the bargain.

Rosalind. You say that you'll have Phebe if she will?

Silvius. Though to have her and death were both one thing.

Rosalind. I have promis'd to make all this matter even:
  Keep you your word, O Duke, to give your daughter,
  And yours, Orlando, to receive his daughter:
  Keep you your word, Phebe, that you'll marry me,
  Or else refusing me to wed this shepherd:
  Keep your word, Silvius, that you'll marry her
  If she refuse me, and from hence I go
  To make these doubts all even.

                    Exeunt Rosalind and Celia

Duke Sr. I do remember in this shepherd boy
  Some lively touches of my daughter's favour.

Orlando. My lord, the first time that I ever saw him,
  Methought he was a brother to your daughter:
  But, my good lord, this boy is forest-born,
  And hath been tutor'd in the rudiments
  Of many desperate studies, by his uncle,
  Whom he reports to be a great magician,
  Obscured in the circle of this forest.

Enter Touchstone and Audrey

Jaques. There is sure another flood toward, and these
  couples are coming to the ark. Here comes a pair of very
  strange beasts, which in all tongues are called fools.

Touchstone. Salutation and greeting to you all!

Jaques. Good my lord, bid him welcome: this is the mot-
ley-minded gentleman, that I have so often met in the
forest: he hath been a courtier, he swears.

Touchstone. If any man doubt that, let him put me to my
purgation, I have trod a measure, I have flatter'd a lady,
I have been politic with my friend, smooth with mine
enemy, I have undone three tailors, I have had four quar-
rels, and like to have fought one.

Jaques. And how was that ta'en up?

Touchstone. Faith, we met, and found the quarrel was upon
the seventh cause.

Jaques. How seventh cause? Good my lord, like this fellow.

Duke Sr. I like him very well.

Touchstone. God 'ild you, sir, I desire you of the like. I
press in here, sir, amongst the rest of the country copu-
latives, to swear, and to forswear, according as marriage
binds and blood breaks: a poor virgin, sir, an ill-favour'd
thing, sir, but mine own, a poor humour of mine, sir, to
take that that no man else will: rich honesty dwells like a
miser, sir, in a poor house, as your pearl in your foul
oyster.

Duke Sr. By my faith, he is very swift, and sententious.

Touchstone. According to the fool's bolt, sir, and such dul-
cet diseases.

Jaques. But for the seventh cause. How did you find the
quarrel on the seventh cause?

Touchstone. Upon a lie, seven times removed:—bear your
body more seeming, Audrey:—as thus, sir. I did dislike the
cut of a certain courtier's beard: he sent me word, if I
said his beard was not cut well, he was in the mind it
was: this is call'd the retort courteous. If I sent him word
again, 'it was not well cut,' he would send me word he
cut it to please himself: this is call'd the quip modest. If
again, 'it was not well cut,' he disabled my judgement:
this is call'd the reply churlish. If again, 'it was not

well cut,' he would answer I spake not true: this is call'd
the reproof valiant. If again, 'it was not well cut,' he would
say, I lie: this is call'd the countercheck quarrelsome:
and so to lie circumstantial, and the lie direct.

Jaques. And how oft did you say his beard was not well
cut?

Touchstone. I durst go no further than the Lie Circumstantial: nor he durst not give me the Lie Direct: and so we
measur'd swords, and parted.

Jaques. Can you nominate in order now, the degrees of
the lie?

Touchstone. O sir, we quarrel in print, by the book: as you
have books for good manners: I will name you the degrees. The first, the Retort courteous: the second, the
Quip modest: the third, the Reply churlish: the fourth,
the Reproof valiant; the fifth, the Countercheck quarrelsome: the sixth, the Lie with circumstance: the seventh,
the Lie direct: all these you may avoid but the Lie direct: and you may avoid that too, with an If. I knew when
seven justices could not take up a quarrel, but when the
parties were met themselves, one of them thought but of
an If; as, 'If you said so, then I said so:' and they shook
hands, and swore brothers. Your If is the only peace-
maker: much virtue in If.

Jaques. Is not this a rare fellow, my lord? he's as good at
any thing, and yet a fool.

Duke Sr. He uses his folly like a stalking-horse, and under
the presentation of that he shoots his wit.

Enter Hymen, Rosalind, and Celia
Still Music

Hymen. Then is there mirth in heaven,
　　　When earthly things made even
　　　　　Atone together.
　　　Good Duke, receive thy daughter:
　　　Hymen from heaven brought her,

Yea, brought her hither,
That thou mightst join his hand with this
Whose heart within his bosom is.
Rosalind. To you I give myself, for I am yours.
To you I give myself, for I am yours.
Duke Sr. If there be truth in sight, you are my daughter.
Orlando. If there be truth in sight, you are my Rosalind.
Phebe. If sight and shape be true,
Why then, my love adieu!
Rosalind. I'll have no father, if you be not he:
I'll have no husband, if you be not he:
Nor ne'er wed woman, if you be not she.
Hymen. Peace, ho! I bar confusion:
'Tis I must make conclusion
Of these most strange events:
Here's eight that must take hands,
To join in Hymen's bands,
If truth holds true contents.
You and you, no cross shall part:
You and you, are heart in heart:
You, to his love must accord,
Or have a woman to your lord:
You and you, are sure together,
As the winter to foul weather.
Whiles a wedlock-hymn we sing,
Feed yourselves with questioning:
That reason wonder may diminish,
How thus we met, and these things finish.

SONG

Wedding is great Juno's crown,
O blessed bond of board and bed!
'Tis Hymen peoples every town,
High wedlock then be honoured:
Honour, high honour and renown,
To Hymen, god of every town!

Duke Sr. O my dear niece, welcome thou art to me,
  Even daughter welcome, in no less degree.
Phebe. I will not eat my word, now thou art mine;
  Thy faith my fancy to thee doth combine.

Enter Jaques de Boys

de Boys. Let me have audience for a word or two:
  I am the second son of old Sir Rowland,
  That bring these tidings to this fair assembly.
  Duke Frederick, hearing how that every day
  Men of great worth resorted to this forest,
  Address'd a mighty power, which were on foot
  In his own conduct, purposely to take
  His brother here, and put him to the sword:
  And to the skirts of this wild wood he came;
  Where, meeting with an old religious man,
  After some question with him, was converted
  Both from his enterprise, and from the world;
  His crown bequeathing to his banish'd brother,
  And all their lands restor'd to them again
  That were with him exil'd. This to be true,
  I do engage my life.
Duke Sr.   Welcome, young man:
  Thou offer'st fairly to thy brothers' wedding:
  To one his lands withheld, and to the other
  A land itself at large, a potent dukedom.
  First, in this forest, let us do those ends
  That here were well begun, and well begot:
  And after, every of this happy number
  That have endur'd shrewd days and nights with us,
  Shall share the good of our returned fortune,
  According to the measure of their states.
  Meantime, forget this new-fall'n dignity,
  And fall into our rustic revelry.
  Play, music, and you brides and bridegrooms all,
  With measure heap'd in joy, to the measures fall.

Jaques. Sir, by your patience: if I heard you rightly,
  The Duke hath put on a religious life,
  And thrown into neglect the pompous court.
de Boys. He hath.
Jaques. To him will I: out of these convertites
  There is much matter to be heard and learn'd.
  (*to Duke Sr.*) You to your former honour I bequeath;
  Your patience, and your virtue, well deserves it.
  (*to Orlando*) You to a love, that your true faith doth merit:
  (*to Oliver*) You to your land, and love, and great allies:
  (*to Silvius*) You to a long, and well-deserved bed:
  (*to Touchstone*) And you to wrangling, for thy loving voy-
    age
  Is but for two months victuall'd. So, to your pleasures:
  I am for other than for dancing measures.
Duke Sr. Stay, Jaques, stay.
Jaques. To see no pastime I: what you would have
  I'll stay to know at your abandon'd cave.   *Exit*
Duke Sr. Proceed, proceed: we'll begin these rites,
  As we do trust, they'll end in true delights.

                          Exeunt all except Rosalind

EPILOGUE

Rosalind. It is not the fashion to see the lady the epilogue: but it is no more unhandsome than to see the lord the prologue. If it be true, that good wine needs no bush, 'tis true, that a good play needs no epilogue. Yet to good wine they do use good bushes: and good plays prove the better by the help of good epilogues. What a case am I in then, that am neither a good epilogue, nor cannot insinuate with you in the behalf of a good play? I am not furnish'd like a beggar, therefore to beg will not become me. My way is to conjure you, and I'll begin with the women. I charge you, O women, for the love you bear to men, to like as much of this play as please you: and I charge you, O men, for the love you bear to women, —as I perceive by your simpering, none of you hates them, —that between you, and the women, the play may please. If I were a woman, I would kiss as many of you as had beards that pleas'd me, complexions that lik'd me, and breaths that I defied not: and, I am sure, as many as have good beards, or good faces, or sweet breaths, will, for my kind offer, when I make curtsy, bid me farewell.

Exeunt